Marco Polo

and the Realm of Kublai Khan

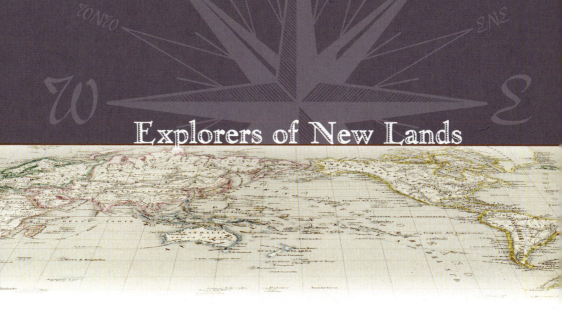

Explorers of New Lands

Marco Polo
and the Realm of Kublai Khan

Tim McNeese

Series Consulting Editor **William H. Goetzmann**
Jack S. Blanton, Sr. Chair in History and American Studies
University of Texas, Austin

CHELSEA HOUSE
PUBLISHERS
A Haights Cross Communications Company ®
Philadelphia

COVER: A portrait of Marco Polo

CHELSEA HOUSE PUBLISHERS
VP, NEW PRODUCT DEVELOPMENT Sally Cheney
DIRECTOR OF PRODUCTION Kim Shinners
CREATIVE MANAGER Takeshi Takahashi
MANUFACTURING MANAGER Diann Grasse

Staff for MARCO POLO
EXECUTIVE EDITOR Lee Marcott
EDITORIAL ASSISTANT Carla Greenberg
PRODUCTION EDITOR Bonnie Cohen
PHOTO EDITOR Sarah Bloom
COVER AND INTERIOR DESIGNER Keith Trego
LAYOUT 21st Century Publishing and Communications, Inc.

A Haights Cross Communications ◀━ Company ®

www.chelseahouse.com

First Printing

9 8 7 6 5 4 3 2 1

Library of Congress Cataloging-in-Publication Data

McNeese, Tim.
  Marco Polo and the realm of Kublai Khan/Tim McNeese.
    p. cm.–(Explorers of new lands)
  Includes bibliographical references and index.
    ISBN 0-7910-8612-7 (hard cover)
  1. Polo, Marco, 1254-1323?–Juvenile literature. 2. Explorers–Italy–Biography–Juvenile
literature. 3. Asia–Description and travel–Juvenile literature. I. Title. II. Series.
    G370.P9M46 2005
    915.04'22'092–dc22
                                                                    2005010060

Table of Contents

Introduction

by William H. Goetzmann
Jack S. Blanton, Sr. Chair in History and American Studies
University of Texas, Austin

Explorers have always been adventurers. They were, and still are, people of vision and most of all, people of curiosity. The English poet Rudyard Kipling once described the psychology behind the explorer's curiosity:

"Something hidden. Go and find it. Go and
    look behind the Ranges—
Something lost behind the Ranges. Lost and
    waiting for you. Go!" [1]

Miguel de Cervantes, the heroic author of *Don
Quixote*, longed to be an explorer-conquistador. So
he wrote a personal letter to King Phillip II of
Spain asking to be appointed to lead an expedition
to the New World. Phillip II turned down his
request. Later, while in prison, Cervantes gained
revenge. He wrote the immortal story of *Don
Quixote*, a broken-down, half-crazy "Knight of La
Mancha" who "explored" Spain with his faithful
sidekick, Sancho Panza. His was perhaps the first
of a long line of revenge novels—a lampoon of the
real explorer-conquistadors.

Most of these explorer-conquistadors, such as
Columbus and Cortés, are often regarded as heroes
who discovered new worlds and empires. They
were courageous, brave and clever, but most of
them were also cruel to the native peoples they
met. For example, Cortés, with a small band of
500 Spanish conquistadors, wiped out the vast

Aztec Empire. He insulted the Aztecs' gods and tore down their temples. A bit later, far down in South America, Francisco Pizarro and Hernando de Soto did the same to the Inca Empire, which was hidden behind a vast upland desert among Peru's towering mountains. Both tasks seem to be impossible, but these conquistadors not only overcame nature and savage armies, they stole their gold and became rich nobles. More astounding, they converted whole countries and even a continent to Spanish Catholicism. Cathedrals replaced blood-soaked temples, and the people of South and Central America, north to the Mexican border, soon spoke only two languages—Portuguese in Brazil and Spanish in the rest of the countries, even extending through the Southwest United States.

Most of the cathedral building and language changing has been attributed to the vast numbers of Spanish and Portuguese missionaries, but trade with and even enslavement of the natives must have played a great part. Also playing an important part were great missions that were half churches and half farming and ranching communities. They offered protection from enemies and a life of stability for the natives. Clearly vast numbers of natives took to these missions. The missions vied with the cruel native caciques, or rulers, for protection and for a constant food supply. We have to ask ourselves: Did the Spanish conquests raise the natives' standard of living? And did a religion of love appeal more to the natives than ones of sheer terror, where hearts were torn out and bodies were tossed down steep temple stairways as sacrifices that were probably eaten by dogs or other wild beasts? These questions are something to think about as you read the Explorers of New Lands series. They are profound questions even today.

"New Lands" does not only refer to the Western Hemisphere and the Spanish/Portuguese conquests there. Our series should probably begin with the fierce Vikings—Eric the Red, who discovered Greenland in 982, and Leif Ericson, who discovered North America in 1002, followed, probably a year later, by a settler named Bjorni. The Viking sagas (or tales passed down through generations) tell the stories of these men and of Fredis, the first woman discoverer of a New Land. She became a savior of the Viking men when, wielding a broadsword and screaming like a madwoman, she single-handedly routed the native Beothuks who were about to wipe out the earliest Viking settlement in North America that can be identified. The Vikings did not, however, last as long in North America as they did in Greenland and Northern England. The natives of the north were far tougher than the natives of the south and the Caribbean.

Far away, on virtually the other side of the world, traders were making their way east toward China. Persians and Arabs as well as Mongols established a trade route to the Far East via such fabled cities as Samarkand, Bukhara, and Kashgar and across the Hindu Kush and Pamir Mountains to Tibet and beyond. One of our volumes tells the story of Marco Polo, who crossed from Byzantium (later Constantinople) overland along the Silk Road to China and the court of Kublai Khan, the Mongol emperor. This was a crossing over wild deserts and towering mountains, as long as Columbus's Atlantic crossing to the Caribbean. His journey came under less dangerous (no pirates yet) and more comfortable conditions than that of the Polos, Nicolo and Maffeo, who from 1260 to 1269 made their way across these endless wastes while making friends, not enemies, of the fierce Mongols. In 1271, they took along Marco Polo (who was Nicolo's son and Maffeo's nephew). Marco became a great favorite of Kublai Khan and stayed in China till 1292. He even became the ruler of one of Kublai Khan's largest cities, Hangchow.

Before he returned, Marco Polo had learned of many of the Chinese ports, and because of Chinese trade to the west across the Indian Ocean, he knew of East Africa as far as Zanzibar. He also knew of the Spice Islands and Japan. When he returned to his home city of Venice he brought enviable new knowledge with him, about gunpowder, paper and paper money, coal, tea making, and the role of worms that create silk! While captured by Genoese forces, he dictated an account of his amazing adventures, which included vast amounts of new information, not only about China, but about the geography of nearly half of the globe. This is one hallmark of great explorers. How much did they contribute to the world's body of knowledge? These earlier inquisitive explorers were important members of a culture of science that stemmed from world trade and genuine curiosity. For the Polos, crossing over deserts, mountains and very dangerous tribal-dominated countries or regions, theirs was a hard-won knowledge. As you read about Marco Polo's travels, try and count the many new things and descriptions he brought to Mediterranean countries.

Besides the Polos, however, there were many Islamic traders who traveled to China, like Ibn Battuta, who came from Morocco in Northwest Africa. An Italian Jewish rabbi-trader, Jacob d'Ancona, made his way via India in 1270 to the great Chinese trading port of Zaitun, where he spent much of his time. Both of these explorer-travelers left extensive reports of their expeditions, which rivaled those of the Polos but were less known, as are the neglected accounts of Roman Catholic friars who entered China, one of whom became bishop of Zaitun.[2]

In 1453, the Turkish Empire cut off the Silk Road to Asia. But Turkey was thwarted when, in 1497 and 1498, the Portuguese captain Vasco da Gama sailed from Lisbon around the tip of Africa, up to Arab-controlled Mozambique, and across the

Indian Ocean to Calicut on the western coast of India. He faced the hostility of Arab traders who virtually dominated Calicut. He took care of this problem on a second voyage in 1502 with 20 ships to safeguard the interests of colonists brought to India by another Portuguese captain, Pedro Álvares Cabral. Da Gama laid siege to Calicut and destroyed a fleet of 29 warships. He secured Calicut for the Portuguese settlers and opened a spice route to the islands of the Indies that made Portugal and Spain rich. Spices were valued nearly as much as gold since without refrigeration, foods would spoil. The spices disguised this, and also made the food taste good. Virtually every culture in the world has some kind of stew. Almost all of them depend on spices. Can you name some spices that come from the faraway Spice Islands?

Of course most Americans have heard of Christopher Columbus, who in 1492 sailed west across the Atlantic for the Indies and China. Instead, on four voyages, he reached Hispaniola (now Haiti and the Dominican Republic), Cuba and Jamaica. He created a vision of a New World, populated by what he misleadingly called Indians.

Conquistadors like the Italian sailing for Portugal, Amerigo Vespucci, followed Columbus and in 1502 reached South America at what is now Brazil. His landing there explains Brazil's Portuguese language origins as well as how America got its name on Renaissance charts drawn on vellum or dried sheepskin.

Meanwhile, the English heard of a Portuguese discovery of marvelous fishing grounds off Labrador (discovered by the Vikings and rediscovered by a mysterious freelance Portuguese sailor named the "Labrador"). They sent John Cabot in 1497 to locate these fishing grounds. He found them, and Newfoundland and Labrador as well. It marked the British discovery of North America.

In this first series there are strange tales of other explorers of new lands—Juan Ponce de León, who sought riches and possibly a fountain of youth (everlasting life) and died in Florida; Francisco Coronado, whose men discovered the Grand Canyon and at Zuñi established what became the heart of the Spanish Southwest before the creation of Santa Fe; and de Soto, who after helping to conquer the Incas, boldly ravaged what is now the

American South and Southeast. He also found that the Indian Mound Builder cultures, centered in Cahokia across the Mississippi from present-day St. Louis, had no gold and did not welcome him. Garcilaso de la Vega, the last Inca, lived to write de Soto's story, called *The Florida of the Inca*—a revenge story to match that of Cervantes, who like Garcilaso de la Vega ended up in the tiny Spanish town of Burgos. The two writers never met. Why was this—especially since Cervantes was the tax collector? Perhaps this was when he was in prison writing *Don Quixote.*

In 1513 Vasco Núñez de Balboa discovered the Pacific Ocean "from a peak in Darien"[3] and was soon beheaded by a rival conquistador. But perhaps the greatest Pacific feat was Ferdinand Magellan's voyage around the world from 1519 to 1522, which he did not survive.

Magellan was a Portuguese who sailed for Spain down the Atlantic and through the Strait of Magellan—a narrow passage to the Pacific. He journeyed across that ocean to the Philippines, where he was killed in a fight with the natives. As a recent biography put it, he had "sailed over the edge of the world."[4] His men continued west, and the *Victoria,* the last of his five ships, worn and battered, reached Spain.

Sir Francis Drake, a privateer and lifelong enemy of Spain, sailed for Queen Elizabeth of England on a secret mission in 1577 to find a passage across the Americas for England. Though he sailed, as he put it, "along the backside of Nueva Espanola"[5] as far north as Alaska perhaps, he found no such passage. He then sailed west around the world to England. He survived to help defeat the huge Spanish Armada sent by Phillip II to take England in 1588. Alas he could not give up his bad habit of privateering, and died of dysentery off Porto Bello, Panama. Drake did not find what he was looking for "beyond the ranges," but it wasn't his curiosity that killed him. He may have been the greatest explorer of them all!

While reading our series of great explorers, think about the many questions that arise in your reading, which I hope inspires you to great deeds.

Notes

1. Rudyard Kipling, "The Explorer" (1898). See Jon Heurtl, *Rudyard Kipling: Selected Poems* (New York: Barnes & Noble Books, 2004), 7.

2. Jacob D'Ancona, David Shelbourne, translator, *The City of Light: The Hidden Journal of the Man Who Entered China Four Years Before Marco Polo* (New York: Citadel Press, 1997).

3. John Keats, "On First Looking Into Chapman's Homer."

4. Laurence Bergreen, *Over the Edge of the World: Magellan's Terrifying Circumnavigation of the Globe* (New York: William Morrow & Company, 2003).

5. See Richard Hakluyt, *Principal Navigations, Voyages, Traffiques and Discoveries of the English Nation,* section on Sir Francis Drake.

The Story
Begins

The year was 1296. Marco Polo, a Venetian trader and merchant, and his crew were once again headed out to sea in the company of a fleet of trading ships from Venice. The voyage he had planned was of no singular importance, just a business trip. His ship, a sailing galley common to the waters of the Adriatic and the great Mediterranean Sea, was loaded with merchandise bound for ports abroad where Polo could buy and sell, as his father had done for years before him. Catching a good wind, the ship's sails billowed, and the galley drew slowly away from the long rows of willow palings that held back the waters of the Adriatic, which posed a constant threat to the floating city of Venice. Polo stood on the galley's deck as he had countless times before through travels that had delivered him halfway around the world. Once again, he was setting sail in search of new places and new people. Perhaps another adventure lay ahead on the water's horizon.

While the purpose of Polo's voyage was common enough, the dark waters that his ship sailed into were dangerous indeed. The seas were filled with enemy vessels. Although they were both Italian city-states, Polo's Venice and its rival trade city, Genoa, were at war with each other. Genoese war ships and armed merchant vessels, like Polo's, were everywhere, scouring the Mediterranean on seek-and-destroy missions. Flying at the top of one of his sails was the Venetian flag, which would signal his port of origin to the enemy.

Perhaps Polo's luck would hold as he set out from his Venetian home. He was, after all, sailing in a convoy of dozens of ships. Perhaps he would sail clear of all the Genoese raiders, engage in buying and selling, and return unharmed, unmenaced, with profit in his purse. He had experienced such good fortune through 25 years of travel, years that delivered him into the court of the great Kublai Khan, the Mongolian ruler of Cathay, or modern-day China. Polo had only returned from his travels to the Khan's court the previous year. His years of exciting adventures and trade with the East had brought him riches and an endless collection of personal adventures, which he was willing to share with anyone who would listen. But on this voyage, Polo's lifetime of good luck would at first appear to have run out.

UNDER SIEGE AT SEA

As his ship sailed along with two dozen other Venetian merchant ships, they were set upon by 15 Genoese galleys. A great sea battle unfolded, and the fleet of Venetian ships was defeated. According to some accounts, the Venetian crews were either

 As Marco Polo sailed with Venetian merchant ships in 1296, a year after his return from China, galleys from the city-state of Genoa attacked the fleet.

killed in the naval engagement or taken prisoner. Marco Polo would be among those captured. Just a year earlier, he had returned from a quarter century of travel across dangerous roads and sea lanes, having faced storms and hostile weather, as well as bandits and warring armies. He had survived each challenge to return to Venice triumphant. Suddenly, however, he was a prisoner of war, bound for a Genoese prison, his fate in the hands of strangers. The once proud court favorite of the Mongol emperor Kublai Khan, Lord of Cathay, might die in an obscure foreign prison, the result of some insignificant and unrecorded battle at sea. In 1296, the world did not yet know the name Marco Polo. Perhaps it never would.

Although Polo had been to Genoa many times before as a trader, he was now entering the city of his enemy under the worst of circumstances. As he was taken ashore along Genoa's waterfront, he watched as stevedores scrambled onto the accompanying trade ships to relieve them of their cargoes. Heavy wagons and carts tumbled down the dock, their beds filled with trade goods in the shape of boxes, bales, and bags. The business of Genoa was little different from Venice, and the dockyard was the scene of much noise and excitement. The Genoese ships had arrived safely, and they carried not only great cargoes, but Venetian prisoners, as well.

Marco Polo was finally taken into the city itself. While his native Venice was a golden, floating city with canals for streets, Genoa was less glamorous, a port town composed of unfortunate-looking houses crowded along narrow, winding streets. The cityscape was interrupted by stumpy towers, which served as private fortresses owned by Genoa's rival aristocratic families. There was little of artistic note, almost nothing of the grandeur Polo was accustomed to in his Venice. Finally, his captors reached the building that would serve as Marco's home for the next three years. Because of his personal wealth as a Venetian merchant, Polo would not be thrown into a dungeon along with the common men whose lives had been spent as sailors and soldiers. He was escorted into the Palazzo del Capitano del Popolo (still standing, it is known today as the Palazzo di San Giorgio), a red stone and brick palace the Genoese had

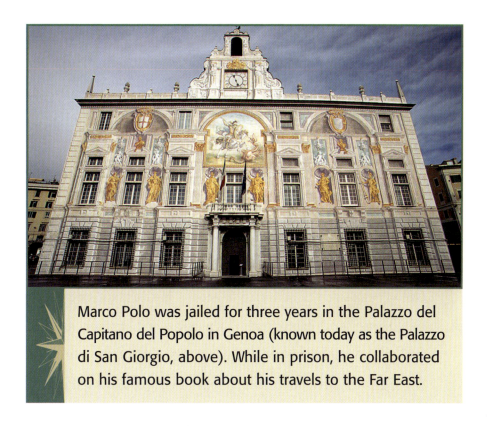

Marco Polo was jailed for three years in the Palazzo del Capitano del Popolo in Genoa (known today as the Palazzo di San Giorgio, above). While in prison, he collaborated on his famous book about his travels to the Far East.

constructed partially out of stones that had once been a Venetian palace in the Byzantine Imperial capital of Constantinople, the spoils of an earlier war between city-states. The Palace of the Captain of the People had been built just a few decades earlier. It was a splendid building with its high crenelations commanding the cityscape above arched windows modeled in the Gothic Venetian style. Polo took no comfort knowing he was to be confined in a building fashioned out of Venetian stones.

BAD FOOD AND VERMIN

The captive Polo found the rooms of his new residence filled with other prisoners, all taken in battles similar to his own. There were Venetians, as well as Pisans, and those from other city-states that had challenged Genoese power. Despite being all Italians, the prisoners did not share a common language, but each spoke his own regional dialect. Classical Italian had not yet been established by the great minds of the Italian Renaissance, such as Dante and Petrarch. The men locked up in the palace, which they all called La Superba, were as foreign to one another as an African was from a Saxon. But within the prison walls, while they did not share a common language, they did share a common experience, one marked by bad rations, poor sanitation, rats and lice, and each a longing for his home.

Despite language differences, the men in La Superba did seek out their own people, those with whom they could share a conversation. In the confinement of the prison, boredom was constant. Anyone who had a good story to tell became popular with his prison mates. Such a man was Marco Polo. He could talk for hours, spinning out tales of the wonderful and the weird, of the foreign and the fantastic. His stories were always set in the lands beyond the sea, off to the East, where black rocks were burned for fuel and everything, or so it seemed, was golden. Polo's stories even intrigued his jailers and prison officials, who went home and told their families of the incredible yarns told by a Venetian, one who claimed to have visited the lands of Cathay. In time, Polo would be treated less as a prisoner, and more as an honored guest of the Genoese.

Among those who listened intently to the stories of Marco Polo was a Pisan, another victim of war, named Rustichello. After hearing Polo tell story after story, he finally suggested that they collaborate and put to paper a written record of the Venetian's fantastic exploits. Polo agreed. Provided with a place in the palace to write, as well as with writing materials, the Venetian and the Pisan were soon busy creating one of the master works of travel history. It would prove to be nothing if not fascinating.

Test Your Knowledge

1 Marco Polo's home city of Venice was at war with
a. Rome.
b. Florence.
c. Pisa.
d. Genoa.

2 The purpose of Polo's trip, during which he was captured, was
a. to explore lands in Africa.
b. to return to the court of Kublai Khan.
c. to conduct business, by buying and selling goods.
d. to battle the Genoese.

3 When Polo was captured, how long had it been since he returned from China?
a. One year
b. Two years
c. Five years
d. Twenty-five years

4 Why didn't the Genoese imprison Polo in the dungeon with the sailors and soldiers?
a. Because of his fame as an explorer
b. Because he knew the warden of the prison
c. Because he was a wealthy merchant
d. Because he had been to Genoa before

5 Rustichello and Polo agreed to

a. come up with a plan to escape prison.

b. create a written record of Polo's adventures.

c. fight for better prison conditions.

d. None of the above.

ANSWERS: 1, d; 2, c; 3, a; 4, c; 5, b.

Birth of an Adventurer

THE MILLION LIES

He was born in a world and a time when most Europeans rarely traveled any farther than 20 miles from the place of their birth during their lifetime. Yet this extraordinary European saw the other side of the globe. He spent years in travel, sailing from sea to sea, and in the company of great camel caravans. He spent nearly 20 years in the court of one of the greatest leaders of the Mongolian Empire—Kublai Khan. His life was an accumulation of adventures. He would become a witness to worlds and people that were so strange to his fellow Europeans. When he finally wrote his life's story, the tales he wove seemed so exotic, so unbelievable, that some called his book *Il Milione*—The Million Lies.

Yet modern historians believe Marco Polo, the great Italian traveler and merchant, to be one of the greatest adventurers of the Middle Ages. He was a man who stepped out of the ordinary and accomplished extraordinary things. His stories of discovery and contact gave Europe its clearest picture of the people of distant lands from Persia to Cathay. His book—*The Travels of Marco Polo*—remained popular for hundreds of years after it was first published. Only through his words could countless thousands of medieval Europeans know of a place where fierce creatures called crocodiles swam in dark waters and strange shells called coconuts grew on tall palm trees. Polo's account of the luxuries and power of the court of the great

Mongol conqueror of China, Kublai Khan, was the only detailed source revealing an otherwise unknown land.

But Marco Polo did more than make a serious contribution to the medieval understanding of the Orient. Modern historians, geographers, sociologists, and scientists credit Polo with other important accomplishments. His descriptions of the Near East and the Far East make him one of the first great geographers of Europe since the ancient Greeks. His scenes of life in Asia serve as one of the first sociological studies in history. He brought knowledge of another world to Europe, information that helped expand the knowledge of those who study the natural world. Over the last 700 years, Polo and the book of his travels remain important subjects of study.

Polo also served as the inspiration for other men and women of adventure, travel, and discovery. Two centuries after Marco Polo's return from his years in the court of the Great Khan, another Italian adventurer set his sights on the Orient. He was from Genoa, a trained mapmaker, and a skilled seaman. He had become convinced that Europeans could sail west across the Atlantic Ocean and reach the distant Spice Islands and golden treasures of the Orient. He knew of the lands of Asia through the writings of Marco Polo. As he set sail in command of three Spanish ships, in search of the riches of the Far East, Christopher Columbus carried with him a book, Polo's book, the inspiration for his own adventures in search of the lands of Cathay.

A YOUTH OF MYSTERY

Although Marco Polo wrote a detailed book about his travels, he never penned a word about his early years. Those who study his life and his travels don't even agree on the year of his birth. Some place it as early as 1251. But most historians believe Marco was born in 1254. Even the place of his birth is in question. He might have been born on the island of Curzola, near the coast of Dalmatia (part of modern-day Croatia) on the Adriatic Sea. His father, Nicolo, and his uncle, Maffeo, had established a trading station on the island. His mother may have been on Curzola at his birth. But most experts are certain he was born in the northern Italian trading city of Venice. Even though his later travels took Marco halfway around the world, he would die in Venice, as well, in 1324.

This building is thought to have been the birthplace of Marco Polo in Venice, Italy. The explorer, however, may have been born on the island of Curzola in the Adriatic Sea.

Little is known of Marco Polo's mother. She died when he was still a boy, but the year is not known. His mother died while Nicolo Polo was on his first trading journey to the Far East, which lasted nine years. Nicolo and Maffeo Polo were important Venetian merchants when Marco was born. They were members of a great council in the city. Their names were included on the list of noblemen of Venice. They traded throughout the eastern Mediterranean region. (Another Polo brother, also named Marco, lived in the important trade capital of the Byzantine Empire, Constantinople. He, too, worked as a trading merchant.)

Through some of the years of his youth, Marco Polo probably lived with one of his father's sisters, an aunt named Flora. Family members raised Marco since his father was sometimes gone for years at a time. He had several cousins, and the young boy probably shared much of his time with them.

Marco Polo probably grew up the same as many other boys in medieval Venice. There was generally little formal schooling at the time. Only the children of the wealthy and aristocratic, like Marco, received much official education. But living in a bustling port city like Venice would have given him special opportunities to learn about the world around him. There was much to learn "in the churches, on the canals, . . . the bridges and the open squares of the city."[1] It is clear that he did learn to read and write. Many young boys in his time remained illiterate. In the first pages of his book on his later travels, Marco tells the reader how, when in China, he "would fix his attention, noting and writing all the novel and strange things which he had heard and seen."[2] Just knowing how to read and write in his own language was more than most Italians in the thirteenth century could do.

Raised as a Catholic, young Marco would have attended church in Venice. He probably participated in the local church festivals and pageants. Marco quite likely enjoyed the special religious holy days, when "great crowds dressed in their best silks, velvets, and furs."[3] He might have walked the corridors of Venice's great church, St. Mark's, which tourists can visit even today. During his youth, skilled artists were at work on the beautiful mosaics in the church. Outside St. Mark's, Marco could have passed by the four great bronze horses in the

Venice, shown above, was one of Europe's most important trading cities in the time of Marco Polo. The city's merchant stalls burst with goods from across the Mediterranean and beyond.

church's portico. They had been brought to the city a few decades earlier from Constantinople, a trade rival of Venice. (Crusaders had raided the Byzantine capital in 1204.) The horses are still there, decorating the outer gallery of the great Venetian church.

THE WORLD BEYOND

But, while there was much to occupy the time of a young boy in Venice, there were other worlds, as well. It appears that young Marco was extremely interested in the sea and sailing. His father traveled

Venice

For a young boy like Marco Polo, Venice was a city filled with wonders. Its plazas were filled with stalls where merchants sold goods from around the Mediterranean and beyond. Goods were delivered by boat, arriving from other coastal ports 1,000 miles away. During the thirteenth century, Venice was one of the most important trading cities in Europe. Some of those faraway ports were connected to the overland trade routes to China, India, Burma, and other exotic Oriental kingdoms. Venice had become a city of great wealth.

Its location was important. The sea-flooded city sat on the northern shores of the Adriatic Sea. From there, it commanded the trade connections between Asia and Europe. Goods from the West and the East came together in the markets of on ships over great distances. During most of his younger years, Marco probably dreamed of his father's return home someday. But he often had to wait months, if not years, before a ship might arrive in Venice with his father onboard.

Venice. Ships could sail from the Venetian port and reach northern Africa, Greece, Spain, Egypt, Turkey, and the southern coastlands of Europe.

Just a few years before Marco Polo's birth, European knights called crusaders had marched off to the Holy Land (modern-day Israel) to fight the Muslims for control of Jerusalem. Venetian shippers gave them passage across the sea. There was so much trade in Venice that nearly everyone in the city was involved in it in some way. Here, Europeans could buy the goods they highly prized, like spices, silks, teak wood, and exotic fruits. There were many people who worked as merchants and shopkeepers. Others owned ships and employed crews who sailed throughout the choppy waters from the Mediterranean Sea east to the Black Sea or west to the Atlantic Ocean.

While he grew up in the middle of this great trade world, he longed to know more about the worlds that merchants like his father visited. The most interesting of all was the mysterious land far to the east that many called Cathay, the medieval name for China. During the thirteenth century, European traders who bought goods from China did so indirectly. That means they dealt with middlemen, traders who lived in lands lying between the Far East and Europe. Many of these connecting traders were Arabs. They dominated the middle leg of the trade by controlling the overland route called "the Silk Road." The Silk Road was actually several roads. It was a 4,000-mile-long network of connecting roads and caravan routes that was used for 1,000 years as the major highway for carrying trade goods among the four great centers of civilization— Europe, the Near East, India, and China.

The cities of China lay at the farthest eastern end of the Silk Road. As goods reached a European port like Venice, stories of this strange distant world were told. Many of them were untrue or were misunderstandings. One such story explained the source of the highly prized trade good, the silks of

China. Venetians were told that it was taken from a type of vegetable or from the bark of special trees. In fact, silkworms produce silk. With each such story, traders longed to know more about the lands of Cathay.

Two Italian merchants became so interested in China that they decided to make a trading journey to the Far Eastern empire. They were Marco's father and uncle, Nicolo and Maffeo. Goods that Venetian merchants bought from other middlemen on the Silk Road or in Constantinople were usually expensive. One reason for the high prices of such goods was that they passed through the hands of many merchants along the Silk Road. As each merchant between China or India and Europe bought and sold Asian goods, he made a profit for himself. By the time a trade item reached Venice, its price was many times higher than it had originally been. Nicolo and Maffeo decided that they could make greater profits if they traveled to China and bought their trade goods directly. They were already trading in Constantinople where they had a trading station. If they could bypass the middlemen, they could make great profits for themselves in the same

Venetian markets in which they had always bought and sold.

When Marco was only 6 years old, his father and uncle set out for the Far East. Their journey would take many years. The brothers were bound for Cathay. They would not return to Venice until Marco was 15 years old.

Test Your Knowledge

1 Marco Polo's adventures and his record of them have contributed in the area(s) of
a. geography.
b. science.
c. sociology.
d. all of the above.

2 Where did the four bronze horses at St. Mark's Church come from?
a. Athens
b. Genoa
c. Constantinople
d. Curzola

3 Which of the following was not connected to the Silk Road?
a. Africa
b. India
c. China
d. Europe

4 One farfetched tale that Venetians heard about the silks of China was that they were made from
a. the feathers of a rare bird.
b. the bark of special trees.
c. the web of a particular spider.
d. none of the above.

5 Why did Marco Polo's father and uncle want to go to China?

a. They wanted to meet Kublai Khan.

b. They wanted to convert the people to Christianity.

c. They thought they could make more money by trading directly in China.

d. They were tired of Venice.

ANSWERS: 1, d; 2, c; 3, a; 4, b; 5, c.

The Polo Brothers

LEAVING VENICE

When Nicolo Polo, Marco's father, set out on his first trade journey to China, Marco was so young, he barely knew his father. His mother was pregnant at the time, as well. But Nicolo and his brother, Maffeo, were convinced that the key to making greater profits in the Silk Road trade was to trade directly with the Chinese. The two brothers knew they would be gone for several years.

The two men set sail from Venice in a boat owned by their trading company. They had loaded the ship with a great supply of trade goods, including all kinds of foodstuffs and other items. They sailed southeast through the Adriatic Sea, around Greece to the Aegean Sea. Then they continued on through waters familiar to both men. They reached their first important destination, the great Byzantine city of Constantinople, without any problems. Here, they sailed on through the straits to the Euxine, known today as the Black Sea. On the northern coasts of the sea, they reached the Crimean Peninsula. As they traveled east, the two brothers traded, adding more goods to their trade list, including a valuable collection of jewels. They knew the great ruler over China, the Mongolian Khan, lived in great splendor and wealth. Such jewels might prove very valuable in their trading efforts.

Once they crossed the Black Sea to the city port of Soldaia (modern-day Sudak, Ukraine), Nicolo and Maffeo continued on overland, purchasing

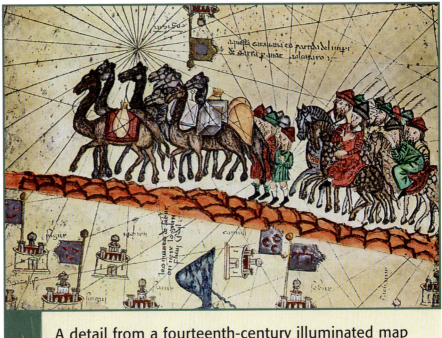

A detail from a fourteenth-century illuminated map shows Nicolo and Maffeo Polo, the father and uncle of Marco Polo. As merchants, the Polo brothers thought they could make more money if they traveled to China and bought their wares directly, cutting out the middleman.

horses. They did not travel alone, but had brought several Venetian servants with them. For many days, they moved east until they reached the court of the powerful leader of the Western Tartars. His name was Berka, and he was the Mongolian ruler in the region, one of the grandsons of the great Genghis Khan. Berka ruled over a kingdom known as the

Mongol Golden Horde. His lands were based in Russia, and included the northwestern quarter of Genghis Khan's empire.

For a Tartar ruler, he was very civilized and open to the arrival of these two European traders to his lands. Traveling in the uncertain world of the thirteenth century, the Polo brothers knew they would have to make friends with men like Berka, or they would not be allowed to continue on the journey eastward. When they met with the Tartar leader, they showed him some of the jewels they had bought along the way. As the Polos realized that the jewels "pleased him, they presented them for his acceptance."[4] Not to be outdone by these gifts from two Italian strangers, Berka gave them presents in return. In fact, he handed them jewels twice as valuable as they had given him. He gave them additional gifts, as well.

The Polos remained in the kingdom of Berka Khan for a year, constantly trading. They may have stayed too long, however. A war broke out over control of the Caucasus region between Berka Khan and another grandson of Genghis, named Alau, who ruled over the Eastern Tartars. In the meantime, the Polo brothers had decided to once again take up their journey toward China. As the conflict expanded, it became unsafe for foreign travelers, like the Polos, to take to the roads. When the civil war ended, the victory went to Alau. Since the Polos had traded with Berka Khan, they decided they could not remain any longer in his defeated state. To avoid the main route and risk capture, Nicolo and Maffeo headed southeast, toward the city of Bukhara, west of the Caspian Sea, in the southern part of modern-day Uzbekistan.

The arrival of the two brothers in Bukhara was fortunate. The city was then part of the Persian Empire and was ruled by a prince named Barak. The city was wealthy, and Nicolo and Maffeo were able to trade for more goods. In fact, they remained in the city for three years. These were years of regional tension and violence, including war. The roads were often not safe for anyone, including foreigners. The brothers had nearly decided to give up their plans to travel to China because of such delays. (The delays did allow the two Italian merchants to learn the Tartar language, however.) But opportunity finally came their way. In Bukhara,

(continued on page 34)

The First Europeans to Reach Asia

When the Polo brothers returned from their nine-year trip to the Orient, they had many stories to tell. They had traveled halfway across the world and become favorites of the Great Khan himself. But their journey to the court of Kublai Khan was not the first time Europeans and Asians had come in contact.

Hundreds of years before the thirteenth century, Europeans and Asians had engaged in trade. Asian goods reached the ancient Greeks by camel caravan and on ships called junks. Oriental spices, silks, and precious stones were bought on the streets of the Roman Empire. Cleopatra, the Egyptian queen who lived in the first century B.C., wore silks imported from China. There was so much trade between the Romans and the Asians that Roman senators tried to limit the amount, fearing that Asian goods were "draining the Empire of its gold."*

After the collapse of the Roman Empire in the fifth century A.D., many of the trade connections between East and West fell apart. Western Europeans had little interest or enough trade items to remain in contact with Asian markets.

Yet there were those Europeans who remained connected to Asia. Some, in fact, traveled to the mysterious Orient. In the larger Asian ports, European traders, as well as Arab merchants, continued to set up shop. A Christian church was built in the seventh century in the Chinese capital at Ch'ang An.

Through the following centuries, Christian missionaries traveled to China and other Asian kingdoms, hoping to spread the word of Christianity. Even as late as the early 1200s, European missionaries, as well as merchants, were living in Imperial China. But by the time the Polos arrived in the Far East, the Mongols had conquered the Chinese.

While much information about the people of the Orient had reached Europe over the centuries, little was known about the Mongols. By the time the Polos completed their travels to these new rulers of China, they added their experiences to those of other Europeans who had, over the centuries, helped to lift the curtain of mystery concerning the wonders of the Asian world.

* Henry Hart, *Marco Polo, Venetian Adventurer* (Norman, OK: University of Oklahoma Press, 1967), 32.

(continued from page 31)

another stranger to the city arrived, "a person of consequence and gifted with . . . talents."[5] He was an ambassador from the court of Alau. He was on a mission to visit the Great Khan of the Tartars, the Supreme Chief, Kublai Khan.

When the ambassador met the Polo brothers, he was quite pleased. He had heard many things about Italian merchants and knew the value of such trading partners. He strongly urged them to travel with him, under imperial safety, to the court of Kublai Khan himself. According to the Tartar diplomat, the Great Khan "would be pleased by their appearance at his court, which had not . . . been visited by any person from their country."[6] The Polo brothers did not hesitate. Traveling with a diplomatic party would make certain that the Polos, strangers in a strange land, would not be harmed.

AN INVITATION TO COURT

With little delay, the Italian merchants joined the ambassador in his journey east. The rest of their trip took another year, as they walked northeast and north. The trip was difficult and included traveling through blinding snowstorms, and crossing mountains and swollen rivers. The party was delayed until the snows melted and the river levels dropped. But in time they arrived in the court of the eastern ruler they had sought out—Kublai Khan. Just as the ambassador from the court of Alau had predicted, the Great Khan was very pleased by their arrival. He honored them with great and fancy dinners. He gave them other honors, as well. The Great Khan had many questions about the home of the two brothers. He knew about Europeans, and asked specifically about "the emperor of the Romans, and of other Christian kings and princes."[7] There were so many questions from the Khan. He wanted to know which rulers were the most important and how large were the lands they held. He asked how they fought their wars and how they carried out justice, and he inquired about the Christian religion. Kublai Khan knew of the Christian faith and wanted to know more about the leader of the Catholic Church, the pope, who came from the same lands as the Italian Polo brothers.

Carefully, the brothers answered the Khan's questions as best they could. They were able to

The Polo brothers are shown appearing before Kublai Khan. Their arrival pleased the Mongol leader, who peppered them with questions about European rulers and the Christian faith.

speak to the Khan in the Tartar language, which greatly impressed the Mongol leader. Soon, the Great Khan became so pleased with the Polos, he asked them to serve him as ambassadors to the pope. They were to take a Mongol ambassador with them, one named Khogatal. The Khan was very interested in making a permanent connection between his court and that of the leader of all Catholic believers. He requested that the Polos ask the pope to send 100 educated missionaries who could teach his court the lessons of Christianity. The Khan also asked for artisans and craftsmen to be sent to teach his people the skills used in Europe. The great Mongol leader had another request. He asked them to travel through Jerusalem when they returned to his court in the future. The Polos were to collect and bring the Khan "some of the holy oil from the lamp which is kept burning over the [burial site] of our Lord Jesus Christ."[8] The Khan believed the oil had special powers. The Polos agreed to all the requests made by Kublai Khan.

Nicolo and Maffeo soon prepared to leave the court of the Great Khan. They were given special letters from the Mongol leader addressed to the pope. They were also given the "golden tablet displaying the imperial cipher."[9] This was their

Kublai Khan presented the "golden tablet" to the Polo brothers before their return to Venice. The tablet was like a safe pass; anyone who had it could travel freely with the Khan's authority.

special ticket back home. The tablet was a safe pass. Anyone carrying such an imperial tablet could journey from place to place with the authority of the Khan. Regional governors would escort such special, privileged travelers through their lands. At any stop, the Polos could use the golden tablet as a blank check and receive any supplies they needed to continue their journey. Later, the royal court of Kublai Khan would pay for everything.

RETURNING HOME

Eager to make their way back home, Nicolo and Maffeo set out, taking their leave of the Khan. But, less than three weeks into their return trip, the Mongol ambassador, Khogatal, fell ill. With his approval, the Polos decided to leave their Mongolian companion behind and continue on. With the golden tablet in hand, the Polos found their return trip much easier and safer. They still faced difficulties, especially with the weather. There was snow, ice, extreme cold and flooding along several rivers. Three years passed before they reached the Armenian seaport of Laiassus, in the spring of 1269. A month later, the brothers sailed on, reaching the port of Acre, on the eastern Mediterranean coast. The two Venetian traders met with a representative of the pope. It was at Acre that the Polos received word that Pope Clement IV had died. Wasting little time and close to home, the Polos took passage on another ship and soon reached their home in Venice.

Nine years had passed since the two Polo brothers left Venice for the court of the Khan. The return of Nicolo and Maffeo Polo was both happy and sad. Nicolo soon learned that his wife had died while he was gone. When his father returned that year, Marco Polo was a young teenager, a 15-year-old boy who had been raised in the homes of friends and relatives. He did not know his father well since Nicolo had been gone for so many years. But the reunion of father and son was the beginning of a new relationship. His father did not wait long to remarry. This meant that young Marco, for the first time in several years, had two parents. He also had "a home in which he was more than a mere nephew or cousin or friend."[10] Marco's father had finally found his way home. But father and son would soon find themselves involved together in an adventure even greater than the Polo brothers had already experienced.

Test Your Knowledge

1 Who was the powerful leader of the Western Tartars?
   a. Berka
   b. Alau
   c. Genghis Khan
   d. Pope Clement IV

2 How long did Nicolo and Maffeo Polo stay in
   Bukhara?
   a. One year
   b. Three years
   c. Five years
   d. Nine years

3 The many delays on the journey allowed the
   Polo brothers to
   a. explore Bukhara thoroughly.
   b. catch up on their reading.
   c. learn the Tartar language.
   d. none of the above.

4 Kublai Khan asked the Polos to return to
   China with
   a. missionaries to teach Christianity.
   b. European artisans who would impart their
      skills.
   c. holy oil from a lamp at the burial site of Jesus.
   d. all of the above.

5 How old was Marco Polo when his father and uncle returned to Venice?

a. 6

b. 9

c. 15

d. 21

Plans to Return

A FAMILY REUNION

With the return of Nicolo and Maffeo Polo to Venice, the direction of Marco Polo's life changed forever. The two Polo brothers wanted to return to China as soon as possible. They had experienced the excitement of an exotic world. Venice did not seem as exciting to them as it had before their travels. They had also made a promise to Kublai Khan to return, this time with missionaries to teach the Christian faith. But their return was delayed by the appointment of a new pope who could provide missionaries. Months of waiting dragged on for the Polos as they grew more eager to return to China.

During those months, Marco enjoyed the company of his father. He had grown into a young man during Nicolo's absence. As a teenager, Marco was likely to be curious about the world and the places his father and uncle had visited. Stories of their adventures must have seemed endless to the naturally inquisitive Marco:

With what eagerness he must have listened to his elders' tales of the strange lands through which they had traveled and the many peoples with whom they had dwelt—their appearance, their dress, their manners and customs, and how their lives and habits differed from those of the Venetians! He probably even picked up a few words and phrases which his father and uncle in all likelihood used at times in their

Venetian speech and stored up practical knowledge which was surely to prove invaluable in
the days to come.[11]

Months of delay passed into two years. Finally,
the Polo brothers decided to return to the court of
the Khan. They were worried that any further delay
might anger the Mongol ruler. The year was 1271,
Marco was 17 years old, and, this time, Nicolo's
departure for the Far East would not result in a
prolonged separation of father and son. This time,
Marco would accompany Nicolo and Maffeo. In
a Renaissance world filled with young men who
never traveled any farther than a day's journey
from their birthplace, young Marco Polo was about
to embark on a journey halfway around the world.
He was about to experience the "thrilling delights
of travel, sightseeing, new scenes, new peoples, new
adventures."[12]

THE JOURNEY OF A LIFETIME

Soon, Marco would leave behind the city of his
youth. Venice had always been his home. He and
the elder Polos visited their relatives and friends

This drawing illustrates the departure of Marco Polo from Venice in 1271. He was 17 years old, and he was accompanying his father and his uncle back to the court of Kublai Khan.

before leaving, never certain they would return from such a long, dangerous journey to the East. That summer, the three Polos set out from the docks of Venice to cross the Mediterranean Sea. Their first destination was the port city of Acre, on the sea's east shores. (Today, it is the city of Akko, Israel.) This City of the Crusaders was a European outpost in the Holy Land. At Acre, the Polo brothers learned of the selection of a new pope, Gregory X. The papacy was willing to provide the Polos with two missionaries, a pair of Dominican friars. Gregory gave his friars jewels and other items to give to the Khan as gifts. He also gave them the authority to appoint bishops and priests from among the converts they would make in far-off Cathay.

While in the city, the Polos requested permission from church officials to visit Jerusalem to buy some of the sacred oil that burned at the traditional tomb of Jesus, which the Khan had requested. Once permission was granted, they proceeded south toward Jerusalem. In the Holy City, the Polos joined an endless throng of European travelers who made regular trips to Jerusalem as pilgrims. A pilgrimage to Jerusalem, to the Christians of the Middle Ages, was a religious experience. There, the Venetian travelers reached the tomb site of Jesus and the purchase of the oil was made.

From Acre, the Polos traveled on to the Turkish port city of Laias (the modern-day city of Ayas, on the Gulf of Alexandretta along the coast of Turkey). From there, they set out toward the East. They made

Pilgrims arrive at the Church of the Holy Sepulchre in Jerusalem, in an image from Polo's book. The Polos visited Jerusalem to buy sacred oil that burned at the tomb of Jesus. Kublai Khan had requested the oil.

connection with a caravan of merchants and camel drivers who were preparing to cross the Silk Road. These merchants traded cargoes of ivory, gold, spices, silks, jewels, and other items. Soon, the caravan crossed Armenia, where the traveling merchant band faced a threat from the local ruler. The Sultan of Egypt had recently invaded Armenian soil and was raiding Christian communities and towns. Since the Polos and others on the caravan were Christians, there was much concern for their safety. As for the two missionaries, they "determined not to proceed further." [13] The Polos would continue on without a single missionary or representative of the pope, "undismayed by perils or difficulties." [14]

The route the Polos took as they journeyed east was a rugged one. The road they followed cut across difficult landscape from the Black Sea to the southeast, toward the Persian Gulf. This route took them across Armenia between the Black and the Caspian seas. From there, they traveled to Tabriz in the northwest corner of modern-day Iran. (Iran was known as Persia in Polo's day.) They passed through the trading port of Laiassus in Cilicia, then known as "Lesser" or "Little Armenia." Today the region comprises part of southeastern Turkey. The port was rich in trade that included spices and cotton. Although many of the locals practiced Christianity, Marco Polo wrote of his disappointment with these people, claiming they were not good Christians. He described the people there as "without any good qualities, but are the best sort of drinkers." [15]

From Cilicia, the party continued on through Turkomania (modern-day eastern Turkey). Along

(continued on page 52)

The Oil of the Sepulchre of the Christ

When the Polo brothers returned from their first journey to the court of Kublai Khan, they soon began making plans to return. One goal was first to buy some special oil in Jerusalem that the Great Khan had heard had magic powers. The oil was the stuff of legend, not only in China, but among Europeans, as well.

By the Middle Ages, the city of Jerusalem was considered a holy site by three religious groups: Christians, Jews, and Muslims. For centuries before the arrival of the Polos in the city, Christians and followers of Islam had fought over Jerusalem. When Christians were allowed access to the city, they flocked by the thousands annually to the Palestinian center to visit places they considered holy. All across the city, places were identified with sites mentioned in the New Testament where Jesus visited or lived. One of those sites was the traditional burial place of Jesus Christ. There, a lamp burned mysteriously. The Khan wanted some of the oil of this miraculous lamp.

The site visited by the Polos and associated with Jesus's burial was a cave that measured about eight feet square. Near its entrance stood a stone, which many claimed to be the stone that had been used by the Romans to seal up the burial chamber holding Christ's body. When the Polos visited the cave, a lamp that hung over the burial site lighted the chamber. According to legend, the lamp was placed in the chamber by two siblings mentioned in the New Testament as friends of Jesus, Martha and her brother Lazarus, whom Jesus, according to the Bible, raised from the dead.

The lamp was said to burn constantly through the year except every spring when "it went out of itself at the ninth hour each Good Friday and lighted itself again on Easter Sunday at the hour of Jesus's resurrection."* It was this "miraculous" oil that the Great Khan had probably heard of and so desperately wanted. When the Polos arrived at the holy site, it was common for pilgrims to buy the special oil. Little did its seller realize that day, as the Polos made their purchase, that some of the legendary oil was to be delivered thousands of miles away to the ruler of Imperial China.

* Henry Hart, *Marco Polo, Venetian Adventurer* (Norman, OK: University of Oklahoma Press, 1967), 78.

(continued from page 49)

this leg of the journey, Marco saw many sights that left him filled with wonder. He and his two relatives passed Mount Ararat, a summit towering nearly 17,000 feet high. It was here that Noah's Ark, from the Bible story found in the Book of Genesis, was said to have rested. The Polos did not try to climb the mountain, since they were part of a caravan, and they were told the top of it was constantly covered with snow. In his writings, Marco Polo noted that the Turkomans, nearly all of whom were Muslims, were "a rude people, and dull of intellect." [16] But he was highly impressed with the region's exceptional breed of horse, as well as its mules, which sold for high prices. It was in Turkomania where "the best and handsomest carpets in the world are wrought . . . and also silks of crimson and other rich colors." [17]

As they traveled on, the Polos heard stories of a strange land to the north, near the Caspian Sea where oil gathered in great pools. Polo called the region Zorzania, which today is part of the Republic of Georgia. Marco wrote that the oil was not used as food, but as a fuel, as well a treatment for skin rashes and other ailments in humans and cattle. The oil fields Polo described are the region of Baku.

Soon, the Polos were passing through territory controlled by the Mongols, the people of the Great Khan. They reached a Christian outpost, the monastery of St. Leonard. The monastery stood on the banks of a large lake known for a local miracle. Normally, the lake seemed empty of fish. But, by the first day of Lent, a 40-day period leading up to Easter, the lake was filled with fish. (During Lent, Christians could not generally eat meat, but were allowed to eat fish.) Then, following Easter Sunday, the fish in the lake disappeared once again. As he traveled through each region, Polo wrote down such stories and did not question their truth.

LANDS OF THE SARACENS

Farther on, the Polos reached the lands of the Saracens, a name then used to identify the Arabs. As the Venetian family passed near ancient Baudas (modern-day Baghdad), they probably skirted around the city. Marco Polo's description of the Muslim town lacks detail. He described it as the site of the "manufacture of silks wrought with gold, and also of damasks, as well as of velvets ornamented with the figures of birds and beasts." [18] In addition,

Baudas was known as a highly advanced city, where the arts and sciences were studied, including physics, astronomy, geometry, chemistry, and optics. Marco repeats tales he had heard that Christians were hated by the local Muslims and that an earlier ruler of the city's region, the caliph, had campaigned to remove all Christians from his lands.

The next city of importance along the route the Polos followed east was Tabriz, a great trading center of the period. Tabriz is, today, in the farthest corner of northwest Iran. The city was filled with many merchants and traders, especially fellow Italians from the city-state of Genoa, who had established a trading colony in the town. With the Persian Gulf a few hundred miles to the south, Tabriz was known as a center for the pearl trade. A contemporary description of the city survives, although it was not written by Marco Polo:

> The city has many beautiful streets and lanes and great market places whose entrances resemble shops. And inside the markets are houses and stores laden with . . . woven stuffs of silk and cotton, sandalwood, taffetas, silk,

and pearls. In one of the arcades of the market place are merchants who sell perfumes and cosmetics for the women. . . . The women are wrapped in white veils and wear horsehair nets before their eyes.[19]

This same eyewitness wrote of how, during the spring, large blocks of ice were placed in the city's wells and fountains, providing ice water for the residents of Tabriz. As the Polos passed through the streets of cities like Tabriz, they added to their stock of merchant goods they intended to deliver to the Great Khan. They traded and bought constantly, as they worked to turn a profit at every turn. As these Italian merchants moved from one region to another, Marco was collecting information and stories. He was also picking up words in a variety of languages, including Arabic, Persian, and local dialects. Slowly, with each passing month, Marco Polo was putting more distance between himself and his home in Venice. The world was becoming his home.

Test Your Knowledge

1 What delayed the Polos' return to the
court of Kublai Khan?

   a. They were waiting for Marco to
come of age.

   b. They needed time to gather
provisions.

   c. They were waiting for the
appointment of a new pope.

   d. They had heard news of civil war
in the Western Tartars.

2 In what city did the Polos buy the sacred
oil from the burial site of Jesus?

   a. Acre

   b. Jerusalem

   c. Venice

   d. Tabriz

3 In Turkomania, Marco Polo was unimpressed
with the people, but was impressed with the
region's

   a. horses.

   b. mules.

   c. carpets.

   d. all of the above.

4 In the land Marco called Zorzania, he observed

a. Noah's Ark.

b. pools of oil, which were used as fuel.

c. the Persian Gulf.

d. none of the above.

5 At the time Marco visited, Tabriz was well known for its trade in

a. carpets.

b. oil.

c. pearls.

d. spices.

ANSWERS: 1, c; 2, b; 3, d; 4, b; 5, c.

The Polos
Journey On

JOINING A CARAVAN

The Polos advanced farther east until they reached the Persian city of Saba, or modern-day Saveh, southwest of modern-day Teheran, the capital of Iran. Here, Marco and the elder Polos were taken to view the burial sites of the Three Wise Men, who visited the infant

Jesus, according to the biblical story found in the Gospels. At the tomb site, Marco saw the bodies and wrote that "they are all three entire with their beards and hair."[20] Marco might have asked the local citizens how corpses more than 1,200 years old could appear to be men who had died more recently. He wrote, however, that "nobody could tell him anything about them, except that the three Magi were buried there in ancient times."[21]

As the Polos continued their journey across Persia, they found a land rich in horses, manufactured goods, silks, abundant grain harvests, and fruit trees and vineyards. The Polos found a special material called "the Turkish stone."[22] It was turquoise, produced in local mines and highly prized by the Persians. (According to Polo, superstitious locals believed turquoise was a sign of bad luck. They thought it was formed from the bones of those who died unhappy because of a failure at love.)

Beyond Saba, the Polos began crossing a great fertile plain until they reached the town of Kerman. There, they joined a much larger caravan of merchants as they prepared to cross the forbidding desert ahead of them. As the caravan moved east, the merchants passed well-fortified towns with tall, thick walls. Such defenses were necessary because a robber band, called the Karaunas, moved through

The Three Magi and the Fire Worshipers

Stories and legends fill the pages of Marco Polo's book recounting his famous journey from Venice to the court of the Great Khan. He heard one such story after visiting the burial site of the Three Wise Men, known as the Magi, who visited the baby Jesus.

The story begins just as the Gospel story of the Magi begins. The Three Wise Men travel from the East to visit and honor the baby Jesus, who they believe will become an important king. They bring gifts of gold, frankincense, and myrrh. The latter two were widely used spices and fragrances in the ancient world.

After the Magi offered their gifts to the Christ Child, the Infant then offered them a gift in return, contained in a sealed box. The Wise Men set out to return to their homes in the East. After a few days, they become curious and opened the gift. Inside the box, they find nothing the region, attacking and robbing everyone they could. It was along this challenging stretch of the journey that the Polo family experienced a fearsome

more than a stone. According to the story, Jesus intended the rock as a symbol for them to remain "as firm as a stone"* in the faith they had gained after visiting Him. But the Wise Men did not understand the symbolism, and, feeling they had been tricked, threw the stone-gift into a nearby pit. Suddenly, the rock exploded in fire. Realizing they had made a mistake, the Wise Men retrieved some of the fire and brought it home. They placed the fire in one of their holy sites, where they began worshiping it.

Marco, in fact, visited a local castle outside Saba just a few days after visiting the Magi gravesite. There he found a small religious sect whose members worshiped fire. It was here that young Polo heard the story of the Magi and of the gift the Wise Men had failed to understand.

* Manuel Komroff, editor, *The Travels of Marco Polo* (New York: Random House, The Modern Library, 1953), 38.

sight. They were caught up in a ferocious, blinding sandstorm. In the violent storm, the Polos took shelter behind their animals, and soon lost sight of the other members of the caravan.

Then, while the storm raged, a band of Karaunas attacked the scattered caravan members. Most of those the Polos had been traveling with were captured and taken away into slavery. Several were put to death. The Polos managed to avoid capture by taking refuge in a nearby castle. With little choice but to continue, Marco and his family members went on south to the port of Hormuz (called Ormus in Polo's book), situated between the Persian Sea and the Gulf of Oman. There, they intended to take a ship and complete their journey to Cathay. But none of the ships in the port were adequate for a long sea voyage filled with the trade goods the Polos had collected during their lengthy travels. Marco described them as "the worst kind, and dangerous for navigation, exposing the merchant and others who make use of them to great hazards."[23] Instead, they turned back toward Kerman, where they returned to the main road that would lead them out of Persia and into modern-day

Afghanistan and a vast desert to the east. For 100 miles, the Polos found no fresh water. Local waters were very salty. Fortunately, they had prepared well, and had adequate food and water for the desert leg of their journey. After passing through this barren, inhospitable land, the Polos and their caravan reached the town of Kobiam.

FROM CITY TO CITY

Polo described the city as "a large town, the inhabitants of which observe the law of [Mohammed]."[24] The city had many iron works and other metal-working shops. In some, they produced large, highly polished steel mirrors. After another journey of eight days through a great desert, the Polo caravan reached the province of Timochain. Here, Marco wrote of towns "well supplied with every necessary and convenience of life, the climate being temperate and not subject to extremes either of heat or cold."[25] It was in this region that Polo also described the people as attractive, referring to the local women as "the most beautiful in the world."[26]

The first significant city the Polos reached next was Balkh, in north-central Afghanistan. The city

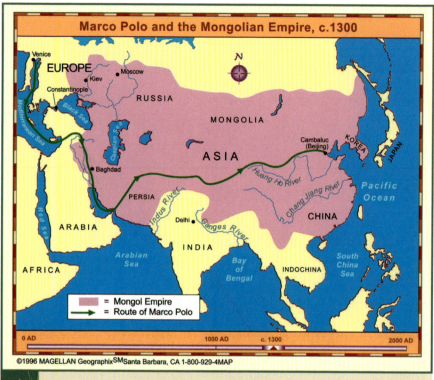

Marco Polo and the Mongolian Empire, c.1300

EUROPE
Venice
Moscow
Kiev
Constantinople
RUSSIA
MONGOLIA
ASIA
Cambaluc (Beijing)
KOREA
JAPAN
Baghdad
Huang Ho River
Pacific Ocean
PERSIA
Indus River
Chang Jiang River
CHINA
Delhi
Ganges River
ARABIA
INDIA
Arabian Sea
Bay of Bengal
INDOCHINA
South China Sea
AFRICA
Mediterranean Sea
Black Sea
Caspian Sea
Red Sea

= Mongol Empire
= Route of Marco Polo

0 AD   1000 AD   c. 1300   2000 AD

©1996 MAGELLAN GeographixSMSanta Barbara, CA 1-800-929-4MAP

This map shows the route that Marco Polo took from Venice to the lands of Kublai Khan.

had been victimized by the Mongols, the people of the Khans. Polo wrote: "It contained many palaces built of marble, and spacious squares, still visible, although in ruins."[27] Wild goats roamed its deserted streets and abandoned fields.

Pressing on, the Polos then reached lands that had been seen by only a few Europeans and written about by none. They soon left the Afghan plains behind as they faced hills to the east. Before them stood, as Polo described it, "mountain after mountain."[28] For nearly two weeks, the party passed along the Pamirs, a high plain stretching across south-central Asia. At this higher elevation, the members of the caravan had difficulty keeping fires going and cooking their food. Through this region, Polo observed other animals new to him, including a breed of large-horned sheep. Because Polo described these curious animals in such detail in his writings, they would later be named for him. The Latin name, *ovis poli*, means "Polo's sheep."

Having crossed the Pamirs, the travelers reached the frontier settlement of Taican, where they found a great wheat market. The surrounding land was fertile, with great almond and pistachio orchards. But the people of the region did not impress Marco Polo. He described them as "an evil and a murderous generation, whose great delight is in the wineshop [where] they are always getting drunk."[29] After leaving Taican, young Polo heard stories of local ruby mines as they passed through the Islamic district of Balashan. He further noted additional mining in the region: "There are mountains likewise in which are found veins of lapis lazuli, the stone which yields the azure color ultramarine, here the finest in the world. The mines of silver, copper, and lead, are likewise very productive."[30]

These same local mountains also held another form of abundance. Marco wrote of the great hunting in the region. Men armed with bows and arrows stalked the hillsides thick with game. There was so much wildlife that the men of the region wore only animal skins. Polo noted that the mountain passes and upland meadows might host herds of sheep as large as 500 or 600 head. In addition, the mountain streams were teeming with trout and many other kinds of fish.

The observant and curious Marco also noted a strange custom of the local women. According to Polo, the women wore extremely large pants or breeches, so large that they required "from 250 to 400 feet of linen, cotton, or silk, thickly pleated and scented with musk."[31] Marco explained that the women covered the lower halves of their bodies with so much material "to show that they have large hips to become beautiful, because in that region their men delight in fat women, and she who appears more stout below the waist seems to them more beautiful and more glorious among other women." [32]

While in this general region, Marco Polo became extremely ill, probably from some type of fever, perhaps malaria. He became so sick that the caravan remained in place for a year, as Marco was unable to travel. During these months, he took several trips into the higher elevations of the local mountains, where the air seemed to help him recover.

As the merchant caravan finally continued on its way, young Polo remained a keen observer of everything around him. He noted the exotic animals, birds, and fish they encountered. He and the other members of the caravan also kept a constant watch out for robbers. Near the province of Scassem, he saw his first porcupines, which he described: "They roll themselves up when the hunters set their dogs at them, and with great fury shoot out the quills or spines with which their skins are furnished, wounding both men and dogs." [33]

MOUNTAINS AND DESERT

After passing through the Pamirs, the Polos reached the distant mountains they had observed for days.

A beacon tower still stands along the old Silk Road in Gansu Province in China. The Silk Road was a 4,000-mile-long network of roads and caravan routes used for more than 1,000 years. The cities of China were at the far eastern end of the Silk Road.

Local Mongols referred to these mountains as the "Roof of the World." Young Marco wrote, "We went over mountains and through valleys in constant succession and passed many rivers and desert tracts."[34] The travel was more difficult here than normal, and the members of the party were relieved when they reached the town of Kashgar, just east of Samarkand. The Chinese name for the town was Shufu. Here, the caravan first entered the lands of China, in the province of Sinkiang. From the local people, Marco Polo began to learn the language that he would need during his prolonged stay in the lands of the Great Khan.

Kashgar was an important trading and merchant city, a crossroads for caravans traveling not only east and west, but north and south, as well. Polo noted the city was filled with merchants from all over the world. All through the region were abundant farmlands, orchards, and vineyards. Farmers raised great harvests of cotton, flax, and hemp. But, as before at other places along the journey, Marco was unimpressed with the local people. He wrote, "But in truth, they are a greedy, sordid race, eating badly and drinking worse."[35]

After their stay in Kashgar, the caravan traveled for more than a week until it reached the borders of Kashmir. Again, he noted the abundance of the land and the beauty of the women. He heard stories of how the locals practiced magic, which allowed them to cause their idols to speak and even change the weather. He also noted how they were independent people, not ruled by an emperor. While here, he came in contact with a curious group of religious men called Buddhists. Their religion seemed quite strange. These holy men lived in great monasteries, followed strict rules, and avoided alcohol and relations with women. Polo noted his disapproval that they appeared to worship idols. But he did admire the fact that they lived to be quite old. The people of the region were neither Chinese nor Mongol. But they were living under the control of the Great Khan.

Onward the Polos pushed themselves, moving from oasis to oasis. They reached Khotan, then Pem; Charchan, then Lop. Although the Polo caravan had traveled a great distance already, it covered another 1,000 miles from Kashgar to Lop. The journey from one city to the next had taken them more than a month. Lop (modern-day Charqliq) was the final oasis before they stepped off into the great, forbidding desert to the east, the Gobi.

For another month, the Polos passed through the Gobi desert with its sandy plains and barren mountains. While the desert was forbidding, the road was well established. As Marco noted:

> At the end of each day's march you stop at a place where there is water—not enough for large numbers, but enough for a hundred persons, and their animals. At three or four of these halting places the water is salt and bitter, but at the others, about twenty, it is sweet and good. Neither beasts nor birds are seen, because there is no kind of food for them.[36]

Polo found the desert crossing difficult, believing that evil spirits haunted the land. He repeated stories of how the desert spirits lured their victims to their deaths:

> If, during the day-time, any persons remain behind on the road, either when overtaken by

The Polos took a month to cross the forbidding, barren Gobi desert. For Marco Polo, the crossing was particularly difficult, for he feared that evil spirits haunted the desert.

sleep or detained by their natural occasions, until the caravan has passed a hill and is no longer in sight, they unexpectedly hear themselves called to by their names, and in a tone of voice to which they are accustomed. Supposing the call to proceed from their companions, they are led away by it from the direct road, and not knowing in what direction to advance, are left to perish.[37]

In an attempt to keep anyone from wandering off, lured by spirits, the caravan attached bells to all of the animals so their presence could always be heard.

After weeks of nervous travel through the dry, inhospitable lands of the Gobi, Marco Polo and his companions reached the town of Sha Chou on the opposite end of the lengthy desert. Here, they encountered, once again, a colony of Buddhists. Sha Chou today is in the Kansu Province. Here, a crossroads brought throngs of caravans together with hosts of worshipers of Buddha. The hillsides were honeycombed with shrines known as the "Caves of a Thousand Buddhas."

The people the Polos encountered were ethnic Chinese, some of the first they had seen in the years since they had begun their journey. Once again, young Marco noted some of the local customs that he considered strange. One was a practice of the

Buddhists. When someone died, they would take paper and cut out figures of items the deceased had owned, such as horses, camels, livestock, even money. The paper effigies were then thrown into a fire and burned, along with the body of the dead person. This, they believed, allowed these items to go with the deceased person's spirit into the next life. Another custom concerning the dead was the practice of breaking a hole in the wall of the deceased person's house. It was considered bad luck to take a dead body out through a door.

THE WORLD OF THE MONGOLS

From Sha Chou, with the end of the journey close at hand, the Polo caravan continued east through the rugged mountains of Tangut to Kansu. The chief trade item in this province of China was asbestos. In this region, Marco heard of a local plant that had been used to make medicines for centuries—rhubarb. Soon, they reached the grand Mongol capital city of Tangut Province, Kan Chou. Many elaborate Buddhist temples, as well as a handful of Islamic mosques and three Christian churches, dotted the city. Nearby, a portion of the Great Wall of China flanked the city. Here, the caravan halted and sent word on ahead to the court of the Great Khan that the Polo brothers had finally returned.

While the Polos remained at Kan Chou, they studied the local customs, as well as the language. Marco noted a local practice of the Mongolians— the drinking of *kumiss*, which was common in western and central Asia. Kumiss was fermented mare's or camel's milk. He describes how the drink was made: "I tell you . . . that they prepare it in such a way that it is like white wine."[38] Polo also describes another form of drink unique to the Mongols:

In case their journey may chance to be delayed by cooking of food and without fruits, but often, for want of wine or water, they live on the blood of their horses, for each pricks the vein of his horse and puts his mouth to the vein and drinks of the blood till he is satisfied; then they stop it up.[39]

In Kan Chou, young Marco took special interest in the local women. Several times during his travels, he noted his displeasure or disapproval of some of the practices of women in some regions. In others, he commented on their great beauty. At Kan Chou, he was impressed with the women and wrote approvingly:

> In my judgment, [Mongol women] are those women who most in the world deserve to be commended for their very great virtue, and they are all the more worthy . . . because the men are allowed to be able to take as many wives as they please. . . . I am ashamed when I look at the unfaithfulness of the Christian women, [and call] those happy who being a hundred wives to one husband keep [their virtue] to their own most worthy praise, to the very great shame of all the other women in the world.[40]

Finally, word came back from the Great Khan. He was ready for their arrival. The Polo caravan continued on, ever closer to its final destination. From Kan Chou, the Polos still had to travel another 60 days before reaching the Great Khan's court. But they were now in the protected company of the

Khan's agents, who would deliver them to Kublai Khan's summer palace at Shang Tu—a place known as Xanadu.

They had spent three and a half years traveling from their hometown of Venice to the far reaches of the Great Khan's lands. They had faced hardships and physical challenges. When they departed from Venice, young Marco had been a lad of 17. He had traveled thousands of miles and learned many foreign customs, as well as foreign languages. He had spent countless days in the open environment, and these experiences had helped him mature into a man in his early 20s. He was older and wiser, and ready for new adventures.

Test Your Knowledge

1 What was the material known as "the Turkish stone"?

a. Gold

b. Opal

c. Copper

d. Turquoise

2 Why didn't the Polos sail from Hormuz to China?

a. They couldn't find enough sailors to travel with them.

b. They couldn't find ships in good enough shape for the long voyage.

c. They didn't have enough money to get a ship.

d. The king forbade them to leave.

3 What type of animal was named after Marco Polo?

a. A type of sheep

b. A type of camel

c. A type of horse

d. A type of fish

4 When Marco Polo became very sick, what helped his condition?

a. A special herb grown in a desert oasis

b. The air in the higher elevations of the local mountains

c. Quills from a never-before-seen porcupine

d. None of the above

5 What is *kumiss*?

a. Horse's blood

b. Mongolian tea

c. Fermented mare's or camel's milk

d. A paste of mashed chickpeas

ANSWERS: 1, d; 2, b; 3, a; 4, b; 5, c.

"Let Him Be Welcome"

THE COURT AT XANADU

The journey of the Polos had taken three and a half years. Those years had changed young Polo dramatically. He had seen new worlds and strange cultures. He had learned other languages. During the journey, his arrival in each new kingdom or city-state helped prepare him for the world of the Mongols. He had met with royal leaders, religious figures, military commanders, and foreign diplomats. Through these encounters, he gained skills that would serve him well.

When Marco finally arrived in the court of the Great Khan, he was 21 years old. Kublai Khan was 60 or 61. Although his father and uncle had told him many stories of the Great Khan and his court, as well as the lands of the Mongols, Marco was stunned by all he saw in Xanadu. For years, the people of Europe had heard stories of the destructiveness of the Mongol warriors. They viewed the Mongols as a ferocious people, bent on destruction. Indeed, Marco and the other Polos had seen the results of Mongol raids as they passed through regions under Mongolian control. They had seen cities that had been destroyed by the Tartar horsemen and the ruins they left behind. But, as he stepped into the court of Kublai Khan, he saw firsthand the splendor of the Great Khan's surroundings, as well as his gentle hospitality.

Young Marco describes the palace of the Khan in rich detail. It was built of marble and other valuable stones. The palace's hallways and its various chambers were golden and elaborate. One large entrance opened toward the city, while the other faced the capital's defensive wall. That wall ran for 16 miles around the palace, and no one could gain entrance into the palace grounds without passing through the palace itself. The palace grounds served as a great park for the Khan and his court, filled with "rich and beautiful meadows, watered by many rivulets, where a variety of animals of the deer and goat kind are pastured, to serve as food for the hawks and other birds employed in the chase."[41]

Marco estimated the grounds to contain more than 200 birds and noted how the Khan went out into his royal park to check on his birds each week. On these weekly inspection tours, the Khan took along a pair of leopards. At his command, the leopards would be released. The large cats would then hunt down a deer or other animal. In the park's center stood a large grove of trees flanked by a royal pavilion, as elaborate as the main palace itself, supported by rows of golden pillars. A dragon decorated each pillar, its tail wrapping around the support column. Its bamboo roof was so highly varnished "no wet can injure it."[42]

An illustration depicts Marco Polo's arrival in China. He first met Kublai Khan at his summer palace, Xanadu. The luxury of the palace, and the Khan's graciousness, amazed Marco Polo.

INTRODUCED TO ROYALTY

Soon after the arrival of the Polos at Xanadu, Kublai Khan summoned them to his palace. He was extremely pleased at their return and excited about hearing of their latest adventures. The Polos presented him with special gifts and official papers from Pope Gregory. Their most important gift was a vessel of the sacred oil from the Holy Sepulchre in Jerusalem, which the Khan had requested from their earlier visit. As Nicolo and Maffeo approached the Mongol leader, the Great Khan noticed the young man with them. Marco was soon introduced by his father: "Sire, he is my son and your man, whom, as the dearest thing in the world, I have brought with great peril and ado from such distant lands to present him to thee as thy slave."[43]

Kublai Khan responded: "Let him be welcome."[44] Immediately, he ordered Marco's name added to the list of those living in his house. From that moment of introduction, Marco Polo "was held of great account and value by all those at the court."[45]

In his writings, Marco presents a description of Kublai Khan, one quite flattering:

The great lord of lords, that is of all those of his dominions, who is called Cublai Kaan is like this. He is of good and fair size, neither too small nor too large, but is of middle size. He is covered with flesh in a beautiful manner, not too fat nor lean; he is more than well formed in all parts. He has his face white and partly shining red like the color of a beautiful rose, which makes him appear very pleasing; and he has the eyes black and beautiful; and the nose very beautiful, well made and well set on the face.[46]

After years of travel, Marco Polo had finally arrived at the seat of power—the court of Kublai Khan. The Great Khan accepted this young stranger, the Polo son, and heartily welcomed him into the circle of power that the Khan embodied. But what Marco saw at the Khan's summer palace at Xanadu would only be the beginning of the many wonders and curiosities that lay before the newly arrived inquisitive Venetian.

Everywhere he turned, Marco Polo faced a strange, new reality. He was introduced to a new form of currency used by the Mongols—paper money. No such thing existed in Venice, or anywhere else in Europe that Marco Polo knew. The money was fashioned from the bark of mulberry trees, stamped with red ink and signed by important officials in the Great Khan's court. Polo noted:

Marco Polo travels with Kublai Khan. The emperor quickly welcomed the young explorer into his inner circle.

This paper currency is circulated in every part of the Khan's dominions, and no person, at the peril of his life, dares to refuse to accept it in payment. All his armies are paid with this currency, which to them is of the same value as if it were gold or silver. It may certainly be said that the Khan has a greater command of treasure than any other ruler in the universe.[47]

To Marco Polo, the more he saw of the Khan's wealth and power, the more it appeared to him that the Mongolian ruler held as much power and importance as any man ever could. As elaborate and amazing as his summer palace at Xanadu was, his primary palace at Cambaluc was even grander. That December, the Polos accompanied the move of the Khan's court back to this extraordinary palace.

LIFE IN CAMBALUC

The capital of the Khan's empire, Cambaluc, was located north of Peking (modern-day Beijing). As the Khan's party approached the capital, Polo noted: "For to this city everything that is more rare and valuable in all parts of the world finds its way. More especially this applies to India, which sends precious stones, pearls, and various drugs and spices."[48] The Polos passed through large, manufacturing towns and the capital's suburbs, where visiting merchants kept their own homes.

As they approached the city, the Khan's entourage passed through an immense gate into Cambaluc. On either side of the gate, a large wall extended several miles into the distance. The royal city measured six miles square on every side, with

(continued on page 90)

The Mongols

When the Polos returned to the court of the Great Khan after several years' absence, they brought Marco along and introduced him to the wonders of an exotic kingdom. Young Polo was spellbound by the luxury, bounty, and elaborate world of the Mongols who ruled China. But not long before, the Mongols had ruled little, and their world had been very different.

Seventy or eighty years earlier, the Mongols were little more than tribesmen living on the grassy plains of Manchuria in northern China. They paid tribute to other tribesmen who dominated them. Polo referred to one of these dominant regional rulers as Prester John, better known as Togrul, the leader of the powerful Kerait tribe.

In time, the Mongolian horsemen grew in numbers until Togrul considered them a threat to his security. He ordered them to leave the Manchurian highlands. They agreed, moving to the north. But the land was inhospitable. Facing death and starvation, the Mongols sought a new leader. One man stepped forward—Genghis Khan.

Genghis Khan first tried a political alliance with Togrul, asking to marry one of his daughters, which would unite the two tribes. Togrul responded, delivering his army to Tenduk, where Genghis had gathered an army, anxious to teach this upstart Mongol leader a lesson.

According to legend, the night before the battle, Genghis asked his astrologers to predict the winner of the battle. The seers placed a stalk of cane upright into the ground. Then, they split the top of the cane and bent the two halves, one toward Genghis's army; the other toward Prester John's forces. They announced that the battle would be won by the side whose cane sprang back into place first. As Genghis watched, his side stood up before that of Prester John's.

As the battle unfolded the next day, the fighting was intense. But, late in the day, Prester John was killed and his army fled the field. Genghis Khan was the victor. Once the Mongols had defeated their oppressors, they launched a campaign of conquest. Within 12 years, they had taken control of the entire region of northern Cathay. Although Genghis Khan died in 1227 during a fierce battle, the Mongolian empire continued. Four Khans ruled in succession after Genghis's death. The fifth ruler was on the throne when the Polos reached China, and he was the greatest of them all—Kublai Khan.

(continued from page 87)

three gates in each of the four walls, which stationed a total of 12,000 guards. "It is not to be thought that such a force is stationed there," wrote Polo, "because of fear of danger from any hostile power, but as a guard suitable to the honor and dignity of the ruler."[49] Once inside the city, Marco saw streets running exactly straight from one wall to its opposite. The streets crisscrossed the urban landscape, creating a squared pattern of intersecting alleyways and thoroughfares. He especially noticed the great Bell and Drum Towers that dominated the cityscape. These signaled the city's curfew, as well as any alarms meant for the people of the city. The bells sounded three times for curfew, and no one was to be seen in the city's streets after that hour, wrote Polo, except "nurses who go for the needs of women in childbirth and physicians who go for the needs of sick men, and those who go for this purpose must carry lights with them."[50]

Once Marco Polo was allowed to enter the palace of the Great Khan in Cambaluc, he was, once again, amazed at what he saw. The palace wall rose to a height of 25 feet. It was thick enough to allow many men to take defensive positions along its top and to

Kublai Khan watches as a deer is chased at Cambaluc, near modern-day Beijing. As opulent as Xanadu was, Marco Polo found the palace at Cambaluc equally extraordinary.

provide housing within the wall for the soldiers manning its ramparts. In wonderment, Marco described this second palace of the Great Khan:

> It reaches from the north to the south wall, leaving only a vacant court where persons of rank and the military guards pass and repass. It has no upper floor, but the roof is very high. The

paved foundation on which it stands is raised above the level of the ground, and a wall of marble is built on all sides and serves as a terrace, where those who walk on it can be seen from outside. . . . The sides of the great halls and the apartments are ornamented with dragons in carved work and gilt, figures of warriors, of birds, and of beasts, with paintings of battle scenes. . . . In the rear of the palace there are large buildings containing several rooms, where the private property of the monarch is kept, his treasure in gold and silver, precious stones and pearls, and his vessels of gold and silver plate.[51]

As elaborate as Marco Polo found the interior of the Great Khan's palace, the Khan's gardens and grounds were equally amazing, just as with the palace at Xanadu. North of the palace stood a great man-made mountain of earth with a base nearly a mile in length. The great mound was thick with beautiful evergreen trees and other varieties. According to Polo, Kublai Khan did not have the trees planted as young saplings. Instead, when he heard of any attractive tree within his kingdom, he ordered it dug up and delivered to his palace mountain, roots and all, with the help of elephants. The massive man-made hilltop forest was known as Green Mountain. In Polo's words, the mountain was "a delightful and wonderful scene."[52] A palace stood at the top of the artificial mountain, the residence of the Great Khan's grandson, Temur, who had been chosen to serve as his heir. (Temur was the son of the Khan's oldest son, who had died prematurely.)

Test Your Knowledge

1 How old was Marco Polo when he arrived at Xanadu?

   a. 15

   b. 17

   c. 21

   d. 25

2 What was Kublai Khan's reaction upon meeting Marco Polo?

   a. He ordered Marco banished from the empire.

   b. He was astounded at Marco's young age.

   c. He immediately welcomed and accepted Marco.

   d. None of the above.

3 The type of currency the Mongols used was new to Marco Polo. What was it?

   a. Paper money

   b. Coins

   c. Credit slips

   d. Coral beads

4 The capital of the empire, Cambaluc, was located near what modern-day city?

   a. Shanghai

   b. Beijing

   c. Hong Kong

   d. Ulan Bator

5 Who were the only people allowed out after
  curfew in Cambaluc?
  a. Soldiers
  b. Guards
  c. Merchants
  d. Physicians and nurses

ANSWERS: 1, c; 2, c; 3, a; 4, b; 5, d.

In the Court of the Khan

ASTROLOGERS AND ADVISORS

At every turn, Marco Polo marveled at the Great Khan's power. He surrounded himself with advisors, troops, women, and a special group, his astrologers. The Khan was a superstitious man and relied heavily on those who were experts at reading the stars. In fact, Kublai Khan had as many as 5,000 astrologers, according to Marco Polo. These men were in his constant employ. They prepared the calendars used by the Khan. They studied the heavens and charted the movements of the stars, the moon, and the planets. Through their studies, they charted weather patterns and tried to predict when it would rain or snow. Occasionally, they predicted even earthquakes. They were responsible for foretelling the arrival of all sorts of potential disasters, from violent storms to outbreaks of disease. The Great Khan expected his astrologers to predict the future, especially his future. As ruler, the Mongol leader had to make many important decisions: where to place his palaces, whether to go to war, when to make a lengthy journey, when to have children. These astrologers served the Great Khan extensively and were very important in giving him confidence in his royal pursuits and decisions.

The Khan relied on his astrologers and other advisors to give him direction not just regarding his personal matters, but regarding his people, as well. By all accounts, the Khan was a benevolent ruler,

Kublai Khan takes a journey with his soldiers. The Khan surrounded himself with troops, advisors, and astrologers. The astrologers, perhaps numbering 5,000, were a special group. Kublai Khan relied on them to predict his future and that of his subjects, as well.

providing for his subjects as well as he could. Annually, he sent advisors out to the people of all the districts under his control. They were charged with finding out whether his subjects in a given province were prospering or suffering; happy or discontented.

If an advisor returned to tell Kublai Khan that the people of a region were suffering because of a drought or flood or other natural disaster, he would not require them to pay taxes to him for a year. If they had experienced a poor harvest, he provided grain to them, charging them only one-fourth of its actual value. To prepare for such famines, the Great Khan ordered regional surpluses bought up by his agents and stored in large granaries for emergency distribution. If a region's shepherds suffered losses among their flocks because of weather or accidents, he would not require them to pay the normal tribute to him of one-tenth of the natural increase in the size of their herds. If lightning or storms damaged a ship, he would not require the usual customs payments on the ship's cargo. Such policies endeared the Great Khan's subjects to him. In Marco Polo's words: "The people all adored him as a divinity."[53]

(continued on page 102)

The Khan's Pony Express

With so many provinces, so much territory under the control of the royal Khan, how was he able to hold his empire together? How could he stay in touch with even the farthest corners of his kingdom? The answer lies in an elaborate communications system.

Kublai Khan, as other Mongol rulers before him, ordered the construction of an elaborate road system, connecting the towns and cities with one another. Along these roads, the Khan dispatched runners, foot messengers carrying dispatches, royal proclamations, and orders to provincial rulers. He also ordered the organization of mounted riders who could swiftly deliver messages over great distances on horseback.

Along the roads, the Khan had foot-stations built, spaced about three miles apart. The runners only ran from one station to the next, then handed off their messages to another runner. This way, all the runners would be fresh and able to cover their assigned distance as quickly as possible. These "royal runners" wore special "girdles" around their waists, with tinkling bells hung on them. These bells announced their approach to the nearest foot-station. This was such an efficient and fast means of delivering the Mongol mail that, according to Marco, "in two days and two nights, the Khan receives news from a distance that in the ordinary way could not come in less than ten days."*

As for the horse riders, they could cover great distances faster than any other means of land transportation of that day. As with the foot runners, a system of post-houses was built, with each house spaced about 25 miles from the next one. Riders would streak on horseback between post-houses, change horses on the fly, and continue their way down the road, delivering important messages and dispatches. Through this system, horse riders would cover as many as 250 miles in one day, riding only during daylight hours. Using this elaborate system, according to Polo, the riders could deliver "news of disturbances in any part of the country, [such as] the rebellion of a chief."** This communication helped keep the Mongol Empire intact by keeping Kublai Khan well informed.

* Richard J. Walsh, *The Adventures and Discoveries of Marco Polo* (New York: Random House, 1953), 43.
** Ibid., 44–45.

(continued from page 99)

A LAVISH LIFE

But, despite his desire to rule his people kindly and responsibly, Kublai Khan spent lavishly on himself and his court. To him, as well as his subjects, he deserved such extravagance. The result was a royal life so pampered and steeped in luxury and excess, it drew constant amazement from Marco Polo. Such extravagance was always part of the great banquets Kublai Khan held in his court.

The two most important feast dates each year were the Great Khan's birthday—September 28—and the arrival of the New Year. On the Mongol calendar, that fell during the first week of February. On the Khan's birthday, each of the provinces under his control was expected to send a valuable gift in his honor.

The New Year's celebration banquet, known as the White Festival, was equally elaborate. All guests wore white costumes, since white was a color of good luck. All gifts to the Khan were to include the color white. The highlight of the great feast was a parade of 10,000 of the Khan's white horses, plus 5,000 elephants. These royal animals were covered with silk stitched with gold and carried containers on their backs filled with golden objects and other valuable items. Marco Polo witnessed such displays of royal wealth and commented with amazement.

At such important feast events, a long table was erected in the Khan's immense dining hall. Married to four wives, his favorite took her seat next to the Mongol ruler, at his left. His sons sat at his right, their table slightly lower than his. At even lower tables sat his advisors, aristocrats, and their spouses, followed by seating for the commanders of royal troops. The guests wore their fanciest clothes to these royal banquets. The aristocracy wore ensembles of golden cloth, ornamented with pearls and jewels. Military commanders wore special uniforms featuring golden belts and leather boots stitched with silver thread. The dinner was sumptuous and ornate. Everyone present drank from golden cups, which attendants watched constantly. They were never to allow the cups to be empty.

Music wafted throughout the dining hall for the pleasure of the Great Khan's guests. There might be dancers or acrobats performing in the great dining hall. Specially appointed servants delivered the banquet food to the tables. Such servants wore silk

The extravagance of Kublai Khan was apparent in his banquets. The guests wore their finest clothes, and everyone drank from golden cups.

cloths over their mouths and noses so they would not breathe on the royal food. At any moment when the Khan raised his drinking goblet, the music stopped immediately, and all those present dropped to their knees where they remained until their ruler had finished his drink.

Every one of the Great Khan's subjects, including his closest advisors, had to recognize the majesty of their ruler. All were to show their respect. Marco Polo noted:

> The order observed by all ranks of people, when they come before his majesty, ought not to pass unnoticed. When they approach within half a mile of the place where he happens to be, they show their respect by assuming a humble, placid, and quiet manner. Not the least noise, or the voice of any person calling out, or even speaking aloud is heard.[54]

In the Khan's presence, this same sort of respect followed precise rules. Anyone visiting the palace was required to remove their shoes and replace them with a pair of special white leather boots before entering the palace, "so that they will not soil the beautiful carpets, of silk and gold and a variety of colors."[55]

Test Your Knowledge

1 How many astrologers did Kublai Khan employ?

a. 5

b. 50

c. 500

d. 5,000

2 The astrologers were used to

a. predict the weather.

b. foretell the arrival of potential disasters.

c. tell Kublai Khan when to have children.

d. all of the above.

3 If Kublai Khan heard that the citizens of a region were suffering from a natural disaster, he would

a. ignore their pleas for help.

b. send his soldiers to restore order.

c. forgive their taxes for a year.

d. none of the above.

4 What were the two most important feast days?

a. Christmas and Thanksgiving

b. The arrival of the spring solstice and the Khan's birthday

c. The Khan's birthday and the arrival of the New Year

d. The arrival of the New Year and the spring solstice

5 What was the color of luck?
a. White
b. Red
c. Blue
d. Black

ANSWERS: 1, d; 2, d; 3, c; 4, c; 5, a.

The Sights of a Mysterious Land

THE WONDERS OF A NEW WORLD

Marco Polo was as observant during his travels and his lengthy stay in the court of the Great Khan as he was amazed by what he saw. As Polo compared the world he had come from to the wonders of the courts of the Khan, the differences made themselves known in all sorts of ways, even to the smallest detail. Traveling along the roads of the Mongol ruler's empire, Polo noted that the Great Khan had ordered trees planted on both sides of the highways. Polo understood why the Khan had done so: "Being only two paces apart, they serve (besides the advantage of their shade in summer) to point out the road when the ground is covered with snow. This is of great help and comfort to the travelers."[56] Marco also noted how roads were marked in regions where the soil would not support tree growth: "When the road lies through sandy deserts or over rocky mountains, where it is impossible to have trees, the Khan orders stones to be placed or columns erected as guiding marks."[57]

In making his observations, Marco Polo noticed a different type of fuel used by the Mongols and the people of China. It was new to him and not widely used in Europe. Polo described the strange, burning fuel: "It is true again that through the province of Catai there is found a kind of large black stones which are dug from the mountains as veins, which burn and make flames like logs . . . and keep up the fire and cook better than wood does. . . . And you may know that these stones are so good that nothing else is burnt through all the province of Catai as far as possible." [58]

As he wrote about coal, Polo noted another curiosity about the people of China: their practice of regular bathing. In Europe, during the Middle Ages, people did not commonly take baths. Months might pass between whole body washings. But bathing was such a constant practice in the Khan's empire, that Marco thought it might one day cause the wholesale destruction of the country's many forests: "It is true that there is no scarcity of wood in the country, but the multitude of inhabitants is so immense, and their stoves and baths, which they are continually heating, so numerous, that wood could not supply the demand. For there is no person who does not take a warm bath at least three times a week, and during the winter daily if possible. . . . The stock of wood must soon prove too little for such consumption." [59]

The Polos were constantly introduced to a variety of exotic foods, all of which were new to Marco. He noted a few in his later writings. One would eventually become a staple in the diet of Italians like Marco Polo: "They do not use bread, these people, but they simply boil . . . three kinds of grain with milk or meat, and eat them. . . . And wheat with them does not give such increase, but what they reap they eat only in strips of macaroni . . . and other kinds of pasta."

In other writings, he describes a popular dairy food: "They have dried milk like unto paste. . . . And when they go forth to war they carry with them about ten pounds of this milk. And in the morning each takes of it half a pound, and puts it in a small leather flask, made like a bottle, with as much water as he pleases. And as he rides his horse the milk in the bottle is churned up and becomes like syrup. This they drink, and it is their meal."[60] This exotic milk product designed for Mongolian soldiers on the go was little more than the equivalent of a power shake. Strangely, although Polo mentions such foods as macaroni and this type of dried ice cream, he never mentions the common drink among the Chinese and Mongols—tea.

AN ASSET TO THE KHAN

With all his powers of observation and his abilities as a quick learner, Marco Polo would prove himself

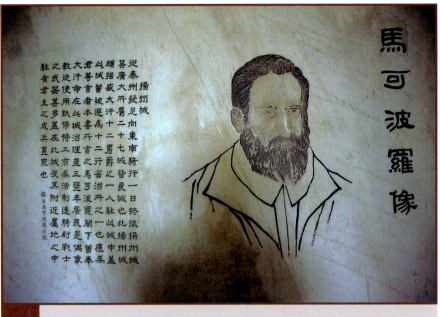

This drawing of Marco Polo, accompanied by Chinese text, can be found in the city of Hangchow, China. Kublai Khan sent Polo throughout his empire to gather information for him. For a time, Polo even served as the governor of Hangchow.

to be a valuable asset to the Great Khan soon after his arrival in the court at Xanadu. With his uncle and father busying themselves in trade and the buying and selling of goods, young Polo had plenty of time on his hands. He set out almost immediately studying and learning the Mongol language. In time, he was probably a fluent speaker. He also studied other languages, those of several of the important foreign ambassadors who lived in the court of the Khan. While modern historians are not certain of all the languages Marco studied, they probably included Arabic, Chinese, and Tibetan.

The Great Khan watched attentively as this young Venetian absorbed the culture, language, and customs he saw around him. He saw an eagerness in Marco, and he sought to cultivate it. With all his other official obligations, Kublai Khan still found time to take an interest in young Polo. Within two years of his arrival in the Khan's court, Marco Polo was appointed as a commissioner of the Khan. In this role, he served as a representative of the Mongol ruler and his court. The Khan sent Polo throughout his empire to visit various provinces to gather information for the Mongol monarch. Anything that might be considered useful for the Khan to know—how taxes were collected, how taxes were spent regionally, how local governments ruled—was fair game for Polo's observant eye. As for Marco and the Polos, his tour of the Khan's empire would give them an opportunity to find out about their prospective markets. By touring the countryside and the cityscapes, the Polos could discover the types of goods needed in each province and what each province might have to buy or trade.

It was a good thing Marco Polo was accustomed to lengthy travel before taking up his duties as a commissioner of the Great Khan. On his first inspection tour, he was sent to the lands of southern Asia, including Burma and modern-day Vietnam. Polo wrote later of his first tour: "The Great Chan sent me, Marco, to remote regions on certain business of his realm (which kept me on the road for a period of four months), and I observed all things diligently which came to my attention either in going or in returning."[61]

Why, surrounded by thousands of capable administrators who were fellow Mongols, as well as Chinese, would the Great Khan entrust such responsibility to a young Venetian like Marco Polo? The answer may be quite simple. There were many who were jealous of the Khan's reign, including both Chinese and Mongols. He did not believe he could trust just anyone who appeared to want to serve him. But the Khan also realized that foreigners serving his court could be corrupt and want to do him harm. Earlier in his reign, before Marco Polo arrived in his court, the Great Khan had employed an Arab advisor named Ahmad. He was a favorite of the Mongol leader and, in the Khan's eyes, the Arab could do no wrong. He gave Ahmad great administrative powers. For 22 years, Ahmad wielded power with a heavy hand, killing anyone who stood in his way. Since the Khan would hear of no criticism against Ahmad, a plot was hatched by a secret society of Chinese to kill the unjust Arab administrator. Only after Ahmad was beheaded, did the Great Khan finally come to know how Ahmad, along with his seven sons, had oppressed the people of his empire. Furious, the Khan ordered Ahmad's body removed from its elaborate tomb and tossed in the street to be ripped apart by dogs. As for his sons, the Khan ordered them skinned alive.

Although Kublai Khan had misjudged Ahmad, he put great faith in young Marco Polo. Polo had proved himself worthy of the emperor's trust and, despite his youth, soon set out on a journey throughout the Khan's lands. Polo's travels exposed him to different cultures and peoples. As he traveled, along with an official party of government agents, soldiers for protection, and other court officials, Marco Polo moved throughout the empire with ease and in comfort. He was a representative of the Khan and was treated well wherever he went. What an extraordinary opportunity this presented for the young Venetian. He was going to be able to see places, people, and customs that few Europeans had ever seen.

PASSPORT THROUGH THE EMPIRE

After leaving the Great Khan's capital, Polo and his fellow officials traveled ten miles to the south to the Hunho River. There, they crossed a bridge that Marco remembered later as a well-built stone bridge, describing it as one "perhaps unequalled by any other in the world."[62] Beyond the river, the party reached the town of Gouza (Cho-chau), known for its fine embroidery. Next, they reached the silk-producing and manufacturing town of Tainfu, where Genghis Khan's enemy, Prester John, had lived in a local castle. Throughout the region, Polo saw many grape vineyards and mulberry trees, which supported worms that produced local silk.

As Polo passed through each province and town, he met more and more of the common people of Kublai Khan's empire. Generally, he liked them and thought they were an admirable people. He considered them highly civilized. As he continued on his journey in the name of the Great Khan, Polo's party reached the Yellow River, which Marco called the Karamoran. He noted that this great Chinese waterway was so wide and deep that no bridge could be built across it. The river, he also knew, flowed into the ocean to the east. But Polo and his party continued on toward the west.

After more than a week's journey, they reached the city of Ken-zan-fu, a provincial capital ruled by one of Kublai Khan's sons, Mangalu. Like his father, Mangalu, according to Polo, "governs his principality with strict equity, and is beloved by his people." [63] Like his father, Mangalu lived in an extravagant palace surrounded by lush gardens and a park. He loved to hunt, just as his father did. Throughout Mangalu's province, manufacturing thrived. Factories produced vast amounts of silk, as well as "every article necessary for the equipment of an army." [64]

Through this leg of his journey, Marco Polo had passed through regions more densely populated and prosperous than most other Chinese provinces. As he continued, he passed into the mountain lands of Hanchung. Here, the landscape held almost no towns and few people populated the region. For weeks, Polo's party saw no one except a few farmers and hunters. Then, they reached the city of Sin-din-fu, nestled near the banks of the Yangtze. The city was one of the most important in southern China. All along the river, Polo noted many ships passing up and down, using the river as a major highway for interior trade.

Past Sin-din-fu, the Polo party continued on into southern Tibet. The local road passed through a thick forest of bamboo. He witnessed a local fire in the forests and was startled when the fire produced loud explosions. Marco claimed he and his fellow travelers could hear the explosions two miles away. Only later did he discover that exploding bamboo canes made the loud cracking noises. Polo and his followers used the local bamboo in their fires at night, since the loud sounds they produced scared off the forest animals that might otherwise attack them in their sleep.

Through this region of Tibet, the party found almost no towns or places supporting inns. As a result, Polo's entourage often had to sleep outdoors. When the party did manage to find a scattering of local people, Polo noted that they were poor and dressed in rags. Soon, the party reached the Yangtze once more and passed into another province, Yunnan.

Using his powers of observation, Marco Polo came to notice a clear difference between the people of northern China and those who lived in the south. Of the southerners, he wrote: "The land is fertile in rice and wheat. The people, however, do not use wheaten bread, which they esteem as unwholesome, but eat rice. Of other grain, with the addition of spices, they make wine, which is clear, light-colored, and most pleasant to the taste."[65]

The party moved on into Burma (modern-day Myanmar), where it reached a lake where local fishermen dove for pearls underwater. Polo heard of local mines that produced turquoise. He also found people who used different types of currency. While some people in the region considered salt as valuable as money, some of the locals used red coral as currency. Women wore coral necklaces to show off their wealth.

Marco and the Great Serpent

Throughout the province of Yunnan, Marco discovered gold was plentiful and could be found in the region's lakes and mountains. Also in Yunnan, young Polo was introduced to a type of creature he had never seen before, which he described later in his writings:

A great serpent lives here. It is a dreadful beast ten paces long and ten palms wide. It has two legs armed with claws in front near its head and its head and jaw are so immensely large that it can swallow a man in one mouthful. By day these animals remain underground because of the great heat, but at night they come out to hunt for food and to drink at the river.*

The animal Marco described was a crocodile. While his details are generally correct, he got several facts wrong. For one, the number of a crocodile's legs.

* Marion Koenig, *The Travels of Marco Polo* (New York: Golden Press Inc., 1964), 41.

Marco Polo's travels through the Khan's empire took him to Southeast Asia, as shown in this illustration. He observed many customs that intrigued him.

He also noted other local customs among the Burmese, including a curious practice involving teeth: "Both the men and the women of this province have the custom of covering their teeth with thin plates of gold, which are fitted with great exactness to the shape of their teeth, and always stay on them."[66]

Passing through the region of thick jungles and forests, Polo mentions several wild animals, including the mythical unicorn. Many people in Marco

Polo's day believed in the existence of a half-horse, half-deer creature with a long, corkscrew-shaped horn on its forehead. If Polo saw an animal he mistook for a unicorn, he was probably referring to a one-horned rhinoceros.

Through Burma he had taken a winding mountain road, much of which would still be in use in modern times. The "Burma Road" became famous and was widely used during World War II. From Burma, he continued his official tour, riding north into the modern-day country of Laos in Southeast Asia. Here he saw more sites and local customs that amazed him, including the practice of extensive tattooing, still common today among Laotians.

Test Your Knowledge

1 What was the strange fuel used by the Mongols that was new to Marco Polo?
a. Wood
b. Oil
c. Coal
d. Tree bark

2 How often did people in China generally bathe in the winter, according to Marco Polo's observations?
a. Every day
b. Every week
c. Every two weeks
d. Every month

3 What languages did Marco Polo probably study?
a. Chinese
b. Tibetan
c. Arabic
d. All of the above

4 As Marco Polo met more of the empire's common people, what did he think of them?
a. He thought they were crooked.
b. He thought they were lazy.
c. He thought they were civilized.
d. None of the above.

5 What was one of the differences Marco Polo noted between the people of northern China and the people of the south?

a. The southerners ate rice instead of wheat.

b. The southerners ate wheat instead of rice.

c. The southerners were not as fond of Kublai Khan.

d. The southerners were poorer.

ANSWERS: 1, c; 2, a; 3, d; 4, c; 5, a.

The Return Home

MISSIONS TO THE EAST

After passing through the northlands of neighboring Vietnam, Marco Polo and his party returned to the capital of the Great Khan, reporting to him all that he had seen and studied. For years, Marco remained an important asset of the Great Khan. The Mongolian leader sent him on many missions "to every part of the empire,"[67] most of which were generally fact-finding trips. As Marco would later write in his famous book, he remained in the service of Kublai Khan for 17 years! During those years, Marco Polo often journeyed to the east coast of China, visiting its ports and cities.

Eastern China was a land of great wealth and power. When Marco and his two relatives reached the court of the Great Khan, the Mongolian leader had not completely subdued the region. In the years that followed, this eastern region, which had been ruled for thousands of years by the Sung emperors, came under the Khan's complete control. When Polo visited dozens of these eastern Chinese cities, he found them extremely wealthy, noting luxury everywhere. For a time, from 1282 to 1285, Marco served as the governor of one of these wealthy Chinese cities, Hangchow (Hangzhou).

During those years, where were his father and uncle, and what were they doing? Curiously, Marco Polo's book says almost nothing about them as he writes his descriptions of his various travels throughout the Mongol-controlled empire. Perhaps, they, too, served the Khan in some way. Marco never fully explains. In at least one edition of his writings, the younger Polo hints that Maffeo and Nicolo remained busy in their constant trading and amassed a significant fortune. Otherwise, the pages of Marco Polo's writings remain silent about his two relatives.

With the passing of the years, the Great Khan and Marco Polo became close friends. He never stopped serving the Khan and remained one of his most loyal advisors. His many journeys kept the Great Khan informed of the state of his vast empire. But as the years slipped by, the Polos began making plans to return to Venice.

Maffeo and Nicolo eventually made their fortunes, having amassed a great quantity of jewels and gold. They were getting older and felt the time had come for them to retire back to Venice. Marco himself had passed from a young man in his late teens when he and his father and uncle had left Venice years ago into his late 30s. The Khan, also, was aging. The Polos had spent years in China living under the protection of the Great Khan, who was pleased by their presence. But, they wondered, what

(continued on page 130)

Marco Polo and Hangchow

During his years of service to Kublai Khan, Marco Polo visited dozens of important cities in the name of the Mongol leader. Few impressed him more than the city of Kinsai, which is today known as Hangchow (Hangzhou).

Hangchow had served as the capital of the Sung, or Song, Dynasty until around 1279, when it fell under the complete control of Kublai Khan. Thousands of years old, Hangchow was called the "City of Heaven" or the "Celestial City." For Polo, it was the greatest city he ever visited. "Its abundant delights," Marco wrote, "might lead an inhabitant to imagine himself in paradise."*

Polo wrote more about Hangchow than any other city he visited. The city was situated between a pristine lake extending three or four miles long and a grand river, which flowed to the sea and the port of Ningpo. Here, great cargoes arrived from India. Near Hangchow, mountains loomed in the distance. On the lake, boats glided along, propelled by boatmen, while passengers indulged themselves in great feasts. Along the river, the boats passed by beautiful palaces and exotic gardens.

In some ways, Hangchow reminded Marco of his home, Venice. The city was crowded and sprawling, with 1.6 million residents. Canals connected with the river ran throughout the city. There were thousands of bridges over these manmade water-ways, as well as brick-paved streets. "Passengers can travel to every part of the province without soiling their feet."** The city's main street was lined with 10 marketplaces. Here, there stood great stone warehouses filled with trade goods from distant lands. Three days a week, each of these markets filled with 40,000 to 50,000 people, who arrived in carts or boats. The stores were an international market of foreign foods, spices, jewels, drugs, wines, and a host of other items. Thousands of merchants and craftsmen worked the markets of the city. Paper currency was widely used.

While Marco Polo, as a Christian, thought of the people of the city as "idolators," he considered them, both the men and women, as attractive, having "fair complexions."*** The women of Hangchow captivated Polo. He described them in glowing terms: "They have much beauty, as has been remarked, and are brought up with delicate and languid habits. The costliness of their dresses, in silks and jewelery, can scarcely be imagined."†

* William Marsden, *The Travels of Marco Polo, The Venetian* (Garden City, NY: Doubleday & Company Inc., 1948), 223.
** Richard J. Walsh, *The Adventures and Discoveries of Marco Polo* (New York: Random House, 1953), 133.
*** Marsden, *The Travels of Marco Polo, The Venetian*, 227.
† Ibid., 228.

(continued from page 127)

if the Khan was to die? Would they be well treated by others in his empire? Since Marco was a constant influence on the Mongol leader, there were many in the court of Kublai Khan who had become jealous of him. Perhaps, the Polos decided, they had better leave while the Khan was still alive.

But, when they asked to leave and return home, the Khan refused. He did not allow them to leave his court for some time. Finally, Marco was able to persuade his master to let them go. The Khan granted permission and gave them the royal *chop*, the golden tablet that would serve as their passport home. The year was 1292.

ONE MORE MISSION

Marco does not describe their return to Venice in great detail, as he would later write of their journey to China. They traveled under the protection of the Great Khan. One reason the Khan had agreed to allow the Polos to leave his kingdom was to deliver a princess to Argon, the king of Persia and a nephew of Khan's whose wife had died. The 17-year-old princess would travel in the company of the Polos, along with a large caravan of attendants and servants. Once again, Marco Polo was embarking on another mission in the name of the Great Khan.

As the Polos set out for Venice, they did not return the same way they had come to China so many years earlier. For much of their journey, they would return by ship. Setting sail for home, their ships traveled south by Vietnam, through the Gulf of Tonkin, inside Hainan Island, to Java, then to Sri Lanka and on to the coast of India. As he had for years, Marco listened to many of the local stories and later recorded them in his journal. When they reached Persia, docking at Hormuz, they received word that the king had died. As a result, the princess was married off to the king's son. While in Persia, the Polos were shocked when they heard the news from China: The Great Khan had died. Before they had left the Khan, the Polos had promised they would one day return. With word of his death, they would never return to China again.

Having completed their mission to deliver the princess to Persia, the Venetians pressed on. Returning as world travelers, the Polos continued to the shores of the Black Sea, arriving at the port of Trebizond. There, they gained passage on a boat

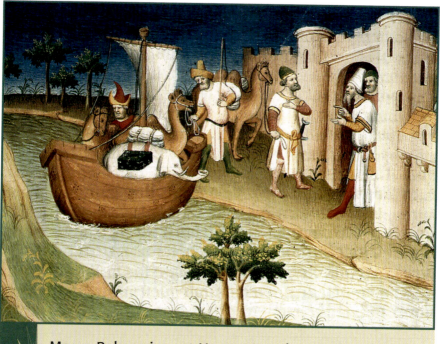

Marco Polo arrives at Hormuz on the Persian Gulf. When the Polos returned to Venice from China, they sailed much of the way home. After they got to Persia, they learned that Kublai Khan had died.

that delivered them to the great Byzantine capital of Constantinople, where they had engaged in trade years earlier. From there, they sailed through the Sea of Marmara, into the great Mediterranean Sea. They finally reached Venice, having completed their long journey. Twenty-four years had passed since a 17-year-old Marco Polo had left his European home and took up a journey in the company of his father and uncle to lands more exotic than he could imagine. He returned to Venice a man of 41 years. In his journal, he described how he and his companions "safely arrived in the year 1295."[68] Joyous at their return, the Polos "offered up their thanks to God, who had . . . been pleased to relieve them from such great fatigues, after having preserved them from innumerable perils."[69] The legendary journey of Marco Polo was complete. Its legacy was, for him, the accomplishment of an adventure that he and, through his writings, the world would never forget.

RECORDING A LEGEND

When the Polos returned to Venice after such a lengthy absence, they were not immediately recognized, even by their relatives. All three men had aged, especially Marco. But once their return was realized, the Polos were soon celebrated throughout the city. Through Marco's stories, Europeans heard, in exquisite detail, about how people lived on the other side of the world.

Some doubted his stories. Perhaps Marco exaggerated from time to time, but many of his tales were of things he had seen with his own eyes. In time, he became known as *Il Milione*— "the man of a million lies." For a while, Marco satisfied himself with only telling stories aloud to anyone willing to hear them. He did not write down the rich descriptions of the sites, people, and cultures he had encountered traveling to and from the Far East.

A year after his return, Marco Polo became involved in a naval conflict between his native Venice and a rival trade city, Genoa. In 1296, he was taken captive after a naval battle that resulted in the defeat of a fleet of Venetian ships. (Marco had been appointed as an honorary commander due to his fame.)

For three years, he remained in a Genoese prison. During this time, he told his stories to a fellow prisoner, Rustichello of Pisa. Rustichello was a romance writer who had written about King Arthur. Hearing Marco tell his stories of his adventures inspired the Pisan writer, and he offered to write down Marco Polo's stories.

The result was a book that became extremely popular across Europe. Originally it was published

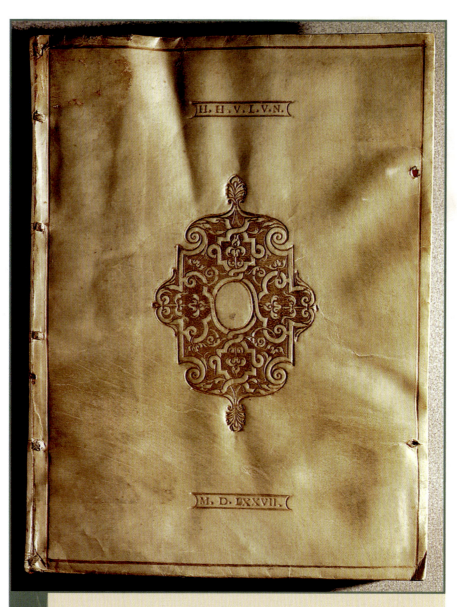

For thousands and thousands of medieval Europeans, *The Travels of Marco Polo* was the only detailed source about those exotic, distant lands stretching from Persia to China.

in a literary form of French, but was soon translated into Latin, Italian, the Venetian dialect, and English, as well as other languages. The English version was titled *Description of the World*. As later versions were copied, retranslated, and recopied, they bore titles that included *The Book of Marvels*, *The Book of Marco Polo*, and *The Travels of Marco Polo*.

While Rustichello may have added some elements to Polo's stories, making them sound more exotic and outrageous than they really were, many historians assumed that much of what was included in the book of Marco Polo's travels did, indeed, happen. As for Marco Polo, he lived enough years after his release from prison in 1299 to see just how famous he was to become through the publication of his stories. He lived another 25 years, married, had three children, and finally died in Venice, in 1324.

Today, there are more than 80 versions of the Marco Polo book written in various languages around the world. The story of Marco Polo remains one of the most exciting travelogues from history. From the beginning, the contents of his book were so amazing that some readers thought Polo had simply made up his many stories. But on his deathbed,

Marco, then 70 years old, was asked to repent if his stories were, in fact, nothing more than lies. The aged adventurer reassured the world with his response: "I have not written down the half of those things which I saw!" [70]

Test Your Knowledge

1 How many years was Marco Polo in the service of Kublai Khan?

a. 3

b. 10

c. 17

d. 25

2 What was one reason Kublai Khan let the Polos leave for Venice?

a. He had grown tired of their presence.

b. They were going to escort a princess who was to marry the king of Persia.

c. He wanted them to deliver a message to the pope.

d. He wanted them to introduce pasta to Venice.

3 When the Polos were in Persia, what news did they hear from China?

a. That Kublai Khan had died

b. That Kublai Khan had been overthrown

c. That Kublai Khan was planning to visit Venice

d. None of the above

4 What did Marco Polo's nickname—*Il Milione*—mean?

a. The man of a million dollars

b. The man of a million adventures

c. The man of a million gems

d. The man of a million lies

5 Who was the prisoner Marco Polo collaborated with on his book?

a. Prester John

b. Rustichello of Pisa

c. Argon

d. Mangalu

ANSWERS: 1, c; 2, b; 3, a; 4, d; 5, b.

1206 The Mongols begin building their empire, taking eastern Europe, Asia, India and China; Genghis Khan comes to power.

1227 Genghis Khan dies in battle.

1251 Kublai Khan becomes governor of China.

1254 Marco Polo is born.

1260 Brothers Nicolo and Maffeo Polo set sail from Venice to the East in search of new trade markets.

1262 Nicolo and Maffeo Polo are caught in a war between two rival Mongol lords; while at Bukhara they are invited to Cathay (China) to meet Kublai Khan.

1206 Mongols begin building their empire; Genghis Khan comes to power

1251 Kublai Khan becomes governor of China

1271 The Polos are able to leave to return to China, and Marco Polo accompanies them

1269 Nicolo and Maffeo Polo return to Venice

1206

1254 Marco Polo is born

1260 Brothers Nicolo and Maffeo Polo set sail from Venice to the East in search of new trade markets

1268 Pope Clement IV dies.

1269 Nicolo and Maffeo Polo return to Venice after nine years. In the meantime, Nicolo's wife has died leaving a son, Marco Polo.

1271 A new pope, Gregory X, is selected; the Polos are able to leave to return to Cathay, and Marco Polo accompanies them.

1274 The first Mongol invasion of Japan ends in defeat.

1275 After nearly four years of travel, Marco Polo, his father, and his uncle arrive in Cambaluc.

1275 After nearly four years of travel, Marco Polo, his father, and his uncle arrive in Cambaluc

1296 Marco Polo is imprisoned at Genoa; he meets a writer, Rustichello of Pisa, and together they begin a book of Marco's travels

1324

1292 Kublai Khan finally gives the Polos permission to leave China and return home

1324 Marco Polo dies

1295 Marco Polo returns to Venice

1279   Kublai Khan establishes the Yuan Dynasty in China; the city of Hangchow comes under his complete control.

1281   The second Mongol invasion of Japan ends in defeat.

1282–1285   Marco Polo serves as the governor of the wealthy Chinese city of Hangchow.

1292   Kublai Khan finally gives the Polos permission to leave China and return home.

1294   Kublai Khan dies; his death marks the beginning of division within the Mongol Empire.

1295   The Polos return to Venice.

1296   Marco Polo is imprisoned at Genoa after the battle of Curzola; in prison, he meets a writer, Rustichello of Pisa, and together they begin a book of Marco's travels.

1299   Marco Polo is released as a prisoner of war in Genoa; around this time, he marries a Venetian woman, Donata, and they go on to have three daughters, Belela, Fantina and Moreta; Nicolo Polo dies.

1324   Marco Polo dies.

1368   The Mongol Empire is destroyed; the Ming Dynasty is established in China, and barriers are erected, shutting off China from the rest of the world for many generations.

Chapter 2
Birth of an Adventurer

1. Henry Hart, *Marco Polo: Venetian Adventurer* (Norman, OK: University of Oklahoma Press, 1967), 43.

2. Ibid., 47.

3. William Marsden, *The Travels of Marco Polo, The Venetian* (Garden City, NY: Doubleday & Company Inc., 1948), 4.

Chapter 3
The Polo Brothers

4. Ibid., 5.

5. Ibid., 6.

6. Ibid., 7.

7. Ibid.

8. Ibid., 8.

9. Ibid., 9.

10. Hart, *Marco Polo: Venetian Adventurer,* 69.

Chapter 4
Plans to Return

11. Ibid., 69.

12. Ibid., 70.

13. Marsden, *The Travels of Marco Polo, The Venetian,* 12.

14. Manuel Komroff, editor, *The Travels of Marco Polo* (New York: Random House, The Modern Library, 1953), 12.

15. Hart, *Marco Polo: Venetian Adventurer,* 82.

16. Marsden, *The Travels of Marco Polo, The Venetian,* 21.

17. Ibid., 21.

18. Komroff, *The Travels of Marco Polo,* 30.

19. Hart, *Marco Polo: Venetian Adventurer,* 89.

Chapter 5
The Polos Journey On

20. Komroff, *The Travels of Marco Polo,* 37.

21. Ibid.

22. Hart, *Marco Polo: Venetian Adventurer,* 91.

23. Komroff, *The Travels of Marco Polo,* 48.

24. Ibid., 50.

25. Marsden, *The Travels of Marco Polo, The Venetian,* 53.

26. Ibid.

27. Richard J. Walsh, *The Adventures and Discoveries of Marco Polo* (New York: Random House, 1953), 23.

28. Ibid., 24.

29. Marsden, *The Travels of Marco Polo, The Venetian,* 61.

30. Ibid., 63.

31. Hart, *Marco Polo: Venetian Adventurer,* 99.

32. Ibid.

33. Walsh, *The Adventures and Discoveries of Marco Polo,* 23.

34. Ibid., 26.

35. Ibid., 27.

36. Ibid., 29.

37. Marsden, *The Travels of Marco Polo, The Venetian*, 73.

38. Hart, *Marco Polo: Venetian Adventurer*, 107.

39. Ibid., 108.

40. Ibid.

Chapter 6
"Let Him Be Welcome"

41. Marsden, *The Travels of Marco Polo, The Venetian*, 99.

42. Hart, *Marco Polo: Venetian Adventurer*, 99.

43. Ibid., 114.

44. Ibid., 114–15.

45. Ibid., 115.

46. Ibid.

47. Walsh, *The Adventures and Discoveries of Marco Polo*, 52.

48. Ibid., 57.

49. Ibid., 58.

50. Hart, *Marco Polo: Venetian Adventurer*, 116.

51. Walsh, *The Adventures and Discoveries of Marco Polo*, 60–61.

52. Ibid., 63.

Chapter 7
In the Court of the Khan

53. Ibid., 67.

54. Ibid., 68.

55. Ibid., 69.

Chapter 8
The Sights of a Mysterious Land

56. Ibid., 45-46.

57. Ibid., 46.

58. Hart, *Marco Polo: Venetian Adventurer*, 121.

59. Walsh, *The Adventures and Discoveries of Marco Polo*, 53.

60. Hart, *Marco Polo: Venetian Adventurer*, 121.

61. Ibid., 124.

62. Komroff, *The Travels of Marco Polo*, 174.

63. Ibid., 181.

64. Ibid., 180–81.

65. Ibid., 191.

66. Walsh, *The Adventures and Discoveries of Marco Polo*, 109.

Chapter 9
The Return Home

67. Ibid., 143.

68. Marsden, *The Travels of Marco Polo, The Venetian*, 19.

69. Ibid.

70. Hart, *Marco Polo: Venetian Adventurer*, 259.

Hart, Henry. *Marco Polo: Venetian Adventurer.* Norman, OK: University of Oklahoma Press, 1967.

Koenig, Marion. *The Travels of Marco Polo.* New York: Golden Press, Inc., 1964.

Komroff, Manuel, ed. *The Travels of Marco Polo.* New York: Random House, The Modern Library, 1953.

Latham, Ronald, trans, *Travels of Marco Polo.* New York: Penguin Classics, 1975.

Marsden, William. *The Travels of Marco Polo, The Venetian.* Garden City, NY: Doubleday & Company, Inc., 1948.

Walsh, Richard J. *The Adventures and Discoveries of Marco Polo.* New York: Random House, 1953.

Yamashita, Michael and Gianni Guadalupi. *Marco Polo: A Photographer's Journey.* New York: Rizzoli International, 2004.

Yule, Henry and Henri Cordier. *The Travels of Marco Polo: The Complete Yule–Cordier Edition.* Mineola, NY: Dover Publications, Inc., 1993.

Books

The Age of Exploration. New York: Marshall Cavendish Corporation, 1989.

Bandon, Alex and Patrick O'Brien. *Travels of Marco Polo.* Orlando, FL: Raintree Publishers, 2000.

Feeney, Kathy. *Marco Polo: Explorer of China.* Berkeley Heights, NJ: Enslow Publishers, Inc., 2004.

Ganeri, Anita. *Marco Polo.* North Mankato, MN: Thameside Press, 1999.

Gefen, Keren. *Marco Polo.* Milwaukee: Gareth Stevens Audio, 2001.

Levy, Elizabeth. *Marco Polo.* New York: Random House, Inc., 1982.

Reid, Struan. *Marco Polo.* Portsmouth, NH: Heinemann Library, 2001.

Riddle, John and Robert R. Ingpen. *Marco Polo.* Broomall, PA: Mason Crest Publishers, 2002.

Websites

The Travels of Marco Polo
http://website.lineone.net/~mcrouch/marcopolo/timeline.htm

Marco Polo
www.encarta.msn.com/encyclopedia_761556866/Polo_Marco.html

Marco Polo and His Travels
www.silk-road.com/artl/marcopolo.shtml

Marco Polo
www.newadvent.org/cathen/12217a.htm

Marco Polo Travel Map
www.susqu.edu/history/medtrav/MarcoPolo/travel.htm

Marco Polo's Asia
www.tk421.net/essays/polo.html

page:

4: © Michael S. Yamashita/
CORBIS
7: © Michael S. Yamashita/
CORBIS
16: © Adam Woolfitt/
CORBIS
19: Snark/Art Resource, NY
29: © Bettmann/CORBIS
36: © Bettmann/CORBIS
38: © Bettmann/CORBIS
46: Foto Marburg/
Art Resource, NY
48: Snark/Art Resource, NY
64: © MAPS.com/CORBIS
68: Werner Forman/
Art Resource, NY

72: © Steve Bein/CORBIS
83: © Bettmann/CORBIS
86: © Bettmann/CORBIS
91: Giraudon/Art Resource,
NY
98: © CORBIS
104: Giraudon/Art Resource,
NY
112: © Michael S. Yamashita/
CORBIS
121: © Archivo Iconografico,
S.A./CORBIS
132: Snark/Art Resource, NY
135: Erich Lessing/
Art Resource, NY

Cover: © Hulton-Deutsch Collection/CORBIS

Tim McNeese is an associate professor of history at York College in York, Nebraska, where he is in his fourteenth year of college instruction. Professor McNeese earned an associate of arts degree from York College, a bachelor of arts in history and political science from Harding University, and a master of arts in history from Southwest Missouri State University. A prolific author of books for elementary, middle and high school, and college readers, McNeese has published more than 70 books and educational materials over the past 20 years, on everything from early American canals to world revolutions. His writing has earned him a citation in the library reference work, *Something About the Author*. His wife, Beverly, is an assistant professor of English at York College, and they have two children, Noah and Summer. During the summer of 2005, Tim and Bev took their own voyage of discovery by taking college students on a 10-day journey along the Lewis and Clark Trail. Readers are encouraged to contact Professor McNeese at tdmcneese@york.edu.

William H. Goetzmann is the Jack S. Blanton, Sr. Chair in History and American Studies at the University of Texas, Austin. Dr. Goetzmann was awarded the Joseph Pulitzer and Francis Parkman Prizes for American History, 1967, for *Exploration and Empire: The Explorer and the Scientist in the Winning of the American West.* In 1999, he was elected a member of the American Philosophical Society, founded by Benjamin Franklin in 1743, to honor achievement in the sciences and humanities.